Kessinger Publishing's
Rare Mystical Reprints

THOUSANDS OF SCARCE BOOKS
ON THESE AND OTHER SUBJECTS:

Freemasonry * Akashic * Alchemy * Alternative Health * Ancient Civilizations * Anthroposophy * Astrology * Astronomy * Aura * Bible Study * Cabalah * Cartomancy * Chakras * Clairvoyance * Comparative Religions * Divination * Druids * Eastern Thought * Egyptology * Esoterism * Essenes * Etheric * ESP * Gnosticism * Great White Brotherhood * Hermetics * Kabalah * Karma * Knights Templar * Kundalini * Magic * Meditation * Mediumship * Mesmerism * Metaphysics * Mithraism * Mystery Schools * Mysticism * Mythology * Numerology * Occultism * Palmistry * Pantheism * Parapsychology * Philosophy * Prosperity * Psychokinesis * Psychology * Pyramids * Qabalah * Reincarnation * Rosicrucian * Sacred Geometry * Secret Rituals * Secret Societies * Spiritism * Symbolism * Tarot * Telepathy * Theosophy * Transcendentalism * Upanishads * Vedanta * Wisdom * Yoga * *Plus Much More!*

DOWNLOAD A FREE CATALOG
AND
SEARCH OUR TITLES AT:

www.kessinger.net

THE BEGINNINGS

OF THE

SIXTH ROOT RACE

(A reprint in more convenient form
of the final chapters of *Man*:
Whence, How and Whither)

BY
THE RT. REV. C. W. LEADBEATER

THEOSOPHICAL PUBLISHING HOUSE
ADYAR, MADRAS, INDIA
1931

FOREWORD

THE following pages are an attempt to sketch the early beginnings of the sixth Root Race, comparable to the early stage of the fifth Root Race in Arabia. Ere the sixth Race comes to its own, and takes possession of its continent, now rising slowly, fragment after fragment, in the Pacific, many, many thousands of years will have rolled away. North America will have been shattered into pieces, and the western strip on which the first Colony will be settled will have become an easternmost strip of the new continent.

While this little Colony is working at the embryonic stage, the fifth Race will be at its zenith, and all the pomp and glory of the world will be concentrated therein. The colony will be a very poor thing in the eyes of the world, a gathering of cranks, slavishly devoted to their Leader.

This sketch is reprinted from *The Theosophist,* and is wholly the work of my colleague.

A. B.

[A very few new paragraphs have been inserted —hardly a page in all; otherwise the book stands as it was originally written some twenty years ago. —C. W. L.]

CONTENTS

CHAPTER I

INTRODUCTORY

THE VISION OF KING ASHOKA

SOME thirty years ago our great President and
I undertook an examination of some of the
earlier lives of Colonel H. S. Olcott. Most
members of the Society are aware that in the
incarnation preceding this last one he was the
great Buddhist King Ashoka; and those who
have read a little memorandum upon his
previous history (written for an American
Convention) will remember that when the end
of that life was approaching he had a time of
great depression and doubt, to relieve which
his Master showed him two remarkable pictures, one of the past and the other of the future.

He had been mourning over his failure
to realize all of his plans, and his chief
doubt had been as to his power to persevere
to the end, to retain his link with his Master

until the goal should be attained. To dispel
this doubt the Master first explained to him
by a vision of the past how the connection
between them had originally been established
long ago in Atlantis, and how the promise had
then been given that that link should never
be broken ; and then, by another vision of the
future, He showed Himself as the Manu of the
sixth Root Race, and King Ashoka as a lieutenant serving under Him in that high office.

The scene of this latter vision was laid in
a beautiful park-like country, where flower-
covered hills sloped down to a sapphire sea.
The Master M. was seen standing surrounded
by a small army of pupils and helpers, and
even while the fascinated King watched the
lovely scene, the Master K. H. entered upon it,
followed by His band of disciples. The two
Masters embraced, the groups of pupils mingled with joyous greetings, and the wondrous
picture faded from before our entranced eyes.

But the vivid impression which it left
has remained undimmed, and it carries
with it a certain knowledge, strange beyond
words and full of awe. The sight which we
were then using was that of the causal body,

and so the egos composing that crowd were clearly distinguishable to our vision. Many of them we instantly recognized; others, not then known to us, we have since met on the physical plane. Strange beyond words, truly, to meet (perhaps on the other side of the world) some member whom physically we have never seen before, and to exchange behind his back the glance which telegraphs our recognition of him—which says: " Here is yet another who will be with us to the end."

We know also who will *not* be there; but from that, thank God, we need not draw any unfavourable deductions, for we know that large numbers who are not at the inception of the Race will join it later, and also that there are other centres of activity connected with the Master's work. This particular centre at which we were looking will exist for the special purpose of the foundation of the new Root Race, and therefore will be unique; and only those who have by careful previous self-training fitted themselves to share in its peculiar work can bear a part in it.

It is precisely in order that the nature of that work, and the character of the education necessary for it, may be clearly known, that we are permitted to lay before our members this sketch of that future life. That self-training involves supreme self-sacrifice and rigorous self-effacement, as will be made abundantly clear as our story progresses ; and it involves complete confidence in the wisdom of the Masters. Many good members of our Society do not yet possess these qualifications, and therefore, however highly developed they may be in other directions, they could not take their place in this particular band of workers ; for the labours of the Manu are strenuous, and He has neither time nor force to waste in arguing with recalcitrant assistants who think they know better than He does. The exterior work of this Society will, however, still be going on in those future centuries, and in its enormously extended ramifications there will be room enough for all who are willing to help, even though they may not yet be capable of the total self-effacement which is required of the assistants of the Manu.

Nothing that we saw at that time, in that vision shown to the King, gave us any clue either to the date of the event foreseen or to the place where it is to occur, though full information on these points is now in our possession. Then we knew only that the occasion was an important one connected with the founding of the new Race—indeed, that much was told to King Ashoka ; and, knowing as we did the offices which our two revered Masters are to hold in the sixth Root Race, we were easily able to associate the two ideas.

So the matter remained until much later, and we had no expectation that any further elucidation of it would be vouchsafed to us. Suddenly, and *apparently* by the merest accident, the question was re-opened, and an enquiry in a department of the teaching utterly remote from the founding of the sixth Root Race was found to lead straight into the very heart of its history, and to pour a flood of light upon its methods.

The remainder of the story is told by him who was chosen to transmit it.

A. B. AND C. W. L.

THE DEVA HELPER

I was talking to a group of friends about the passage in the *Jñāneshvari* which describes the yogī as " hearing and comprehending the language of the Devas," and trying to explain in what wonderful ecstasies of colour and sound certain orders of the great Angels express themselves, when I was aware of the presence of one of them, who has on several previous occasions been good enough to give me some help in my efforts to understand the mysteries of their glorious existence. Seeing, I suppose, the inadequacy of my attempts at description, he put before me two singularly vivid little pictures, and said to me : " There, describe this to them."

Each of the pictures showed the interior of a great Temple, of architecture unlike any with which I am familiar, and in each a Deva was acting as priest or minister, and leading the devotions of a vast congregation. In one of these the officiant was producing his results entirely by the manipulation of an indescribably splendid display of colours, while in the other case music was the medium through which he on the one hand appealed to the emotions of his congregation, and on the other expressed their aspirations to the Deity.

A more detailed description of these Temples and of the methods adopted in them will be given later ; for the moment let us pass on to the further investigations of which this was only the starting-point. The Deva who showed these pictures explained that they represented scenes from a future in which Devas would move far more freely among men than they do at present, and would help them not only in their devotions but also in many other ways. Thanking him for his kind assistance, I described the lovely pictures as well as I could to my group, he himself making occasional suggestions.

SEEING THE FUTURE

When the meeting was over, in the privacy of my chamber I recalled these pictures with the greatest pleasure, fixed them upon my mind in the minutest detail, and endeavoured to discover how far it was possible to see in connection with them other surrounding circumstances. To my great delight, I found that this was perfectly possible—that I could, by an effort, extend my vision from the Temples to the town and country surrounding them, and could in this way see and describe in detail this life of the future.

This naturally raises a host of questions as to the type of clairvoyance by which the future is thus foreseen, the extent to which such future may be thought of as fore-ordained, and how far, if at all, what is seen is modifiable by the wills of those who are observed as actors in the drama ; for if all is already arranged, and they cannot change it, are we not once more face to face with the wearisome theory of predestination ? I am no more competent to settle satisfactorily the question of free-will and predestination than any of the thousands of people who have written upon it, but at least I can bear testimony to one undoubted fact— that there *is* a plane from which the past, the present, and the future have lost their relative characteristics, and each is as actually and absolutely present in consciousness as the others.

I have in many cases examined the records of the past, and have more than once described how utterly real and living those records are to the investigator. He is simply living in the scene, and he can train himself to look upon it from the outside merely as a spectator, or to identify his consciousness for the time with that of some person who is taking part in that scene, and so have the great advantage of contemporary opinion on the subject under review.

I can only say that in this, the first long and connected vision of the future which I have undertaken, the experience was precisely similar; that this future also was in every way as actual, as vividly present, as any of those scenes of the past, or as the room in which I sit as I write; that in this case also precisely the same two possibilities existed—that of looking on the whole thing as a spectator, or of identifying oneself with the consciousness of one who was living in it, and thereby realizing exactly what were his motives and how life appeared to him.

As, during part of the investigation, I happened to have present with me in the physical body one of those whom I clearly saw taking part in that community of the future, I made some special effort to see how far it may be possible for that ego, by action in the intervening centuries, to prevent himself from taking part in that movement or to modify his attitude with regard to it. It seemed clear to me, after repeated and most careful exmina-tion, that he can *not* avoid or appreciably modify this destiny which lies before him; but the reason that he cannot do this is that the Monad above him, the very Spirit within him, acting through the as yet undeveloped part of himself as an ego, has already deter-mined upon this, and set in motion the causes which must inevitably produce it. The ego has unquestionably a large amount of freedom in these intervening centuries. He can move aside from the path marked out for him to this side or to that; he can hurry his progress along it or delay it; but yet the inexorable compelling power (which is still at the same time his truest Self) will not permit such absolute and final divergence from it as might cause him to lose the opportunity which lies before him. The Will of the true man is already set, and that Will will certainly prevail.

I know very well the exceeding difficulty of thought upon this subject, and I am not in the least presuming to propound any new solution for it; I am simply offering a contribution to the study of the subject in the shape of a piece of testimony. Let it be sufficient for the moment to state that I for my part know this to be an accurate picture of what will inevitably happen; and, knowing that, I put it thus before our readers as a matter which I think will be of deep interest to them and a great encouragement to those who find themselves able to accept it; while at the same time I have not the slightest wish to press it upon the notice of those who have not as yet acquired the certainty that it is possible to foresee the distant future even in the minutest detail.

CHAPTER II

THE COMMUNITY

IT was discovered that these gorgeous Temple services do not represent what will be the ordinary worship of the world at that period, but that they will take place among a certain community of persons living apart from the rest of the world; and but little further research was necessary to show us that this is the very same community, the foundation of which had formed the basis of the vision shown so long ago to King Ashoka. This community is in fact the segregation made by the Manu of the sixth Root Race; but instead of carrying it away into remote desert places inaccessible to the rest of the world—as did the Manu of the fifth Root Race—our Manu plants it in the midst of a populous country, and preserves it from admixture with earlier races by a moral boundary only.

Just as the material for the *fifth* Root Race had to be taken from the *fifth* sub-race of the Atlantean stock, so the material bodies from which the *sixth* Root Race is to be developed are to be selected from the *sixth* sub-race of our present Āryan Race. It is therefore perfectly natural that this community should be established, as it was found to be, on the great continent of North America, where even already steps are being taken towards the development of the sixth sub-race. Equally natural is it that the part of that continent chosen should be that which in scenery and climate approaches most nearly to our ideal of Paradise, that is to say, Lower California. It is found that the date of the events portrayed in the vision of King Ashoka—the actual founding of the community—is about seven hundred years from the present time ; but the pictures shown by the Deva (and those revealed by the investigations which sprang from them) belong to a period, about one hundred and fifty years later, when the community is already thoroughly established and fully self-reliant.

FOUNDING THE COMMUNITY

The plan is this. From the Theosophical Society as it is now, and as it will be in the centuries to come, the Manu and the High-Priest of the coming Race—named Mars and Mercury in the list of characters who appear in *The Lives of Alcyone*—select such people as are thoroughly in earnest and devoted to Their service, and offer to them the opportunity of becoming Their assistants in this great work. It is not to be denied that the work will be arduous, and that it will require the utmost sacrifice on the part of those who are privileged to share in it.

The LOGOS, before He called into existence this part of His system, had in His mind a detailed plan of what He intended to do with it —to what level each Race in each Round should attain, and in what particulars it must differ from its predecessors. The whole of His mighty thought-form exists even now upon the plane of the Divine Mind; and when a Manu is appointed to take charge of a Root Race, His first proceeding is to materialize this thought-form down to some plane where

He can have it at hand for ready reference. His task is then to take from the existing world such men as most nearly resemble this type, to draw them apart from the rest, and gradually to develop in them, so far as may be, the qualities which are to be specially characteristic of the new Race.

When He has carried this process as far as He thinks possible with the material ready to His hand, He will Himself incarnate in the segregated group. Since He has long ago exhausted all hindering karma, He is perfectly free to mould all His vehicles, causal, mental and astral, exactly to the copy set before Him by the LOGOS. No doubt He can also exercise a great influence even upon His physical vehicle, though He must owe that to parents who, after all, belong still to the fifth Root Race, even though themselves specialized to a large extent.

Only those bodies which are physically descended in a direct line from Him constitute the new Root Race; and since He in His turn must obviously marry into the old fifth Root Race, it is clear that the type will not be absolutely pure. For the first generation His children must also take to themselves partners from the old Race, though only within the limits of the segregated group ; but after that generation there is no further admixture of the older blood, intermarriage outside of the newly constituted family being absolutely forbidden.   Later on, the Manu Himself will re-incarnate, probably as His own great-grandchild, and so will further purify the Race, and all the while He will never relax His efforts to mould all their vehicles, now including even the physical, into closer and closer resemblance to the model given to Him by the LOGOS.

GATHERING THE MEMBERS

In order that this work of special moulding should be done as quickly and as completely as possible, it is eminently necessary that all the egos incarnating in these new vehicles should themselves fully understand what is being done, and be utterly devoted to the work. Therefore the Manu gathers round Him for this purpose a large number of His pupils and helpers, and puts them into the bodies which

He Himself provides, the arrangement being that they shall wholly dedicate themselves to this task, taking up a new body as soon as they find it necessary to lay aside the old one.

Therefore, as we have said, exceedingly arduous labour will be involved for those who become His assistants; they must take birth again and again without the usual interval on other planes; and further, every one of this unbroken string of physical lives must be absolutely unselfish—must be entirely consecrated to the interests of the new Race without the slightest thought of self or of personal interest. In fact, the man who undertakes this must live not for himself but for the Race, and this for century after century.

This is no light burden to assume; but on the other side of the account it must be said that those who undertake it will inevitably make abnormally rapid progress, and will have not only the glory of taking a leading part in the evolution of humanity, but also the inestimable privilege of working through many lives under the immediate physical

2

direction of the Masters whom they love so dearly. And those who have already been so blest as to taste the sweetness of Their presence know well that in that presence no labour seems arduous, no obstacles seem insurmountable; rather all difficulties vanish, and we look back in wonder at the stumbles of yesterday, finding it impossible to comprehend how we could have felt discouraged or despairing. The feeling is exactly that which the Apostle so well expressed when he said: "I can do all things through Christ which strengtheneth me."

ENTERING THE ESTATE

When the time draws near which in His judgment is the most suitable for the actual founding of the Race, He will see to it that all these disciples whom He has selected shall take birth in that sixth sub-race. When they have all attained maturity He (or they jointly) will purchase a large estate in a convenient spot, and all will journey thither and commence their new life as a community. It was this scene of the taking possession of the estate which was shown to King Ashoka, and the particular spot at which the two Masters were seen to meet is one near the boundary of the estate.

They then lead Their followers to the central site which has already been selected for the principal city of the community, and there they take possession of the dwellings which have been previously prepared for them. For, long before this, the Manu and His immediate lieutenants have supervised the erection of a magnificent group of buildings in preparation for this occasion—a great central Temple or cathedral, vast buildings arranged as libraries, museums and council-halls, and, surrounding these, perhaps some four hundred dwelling-houses, each standing in the midst of its own plot of ground. Though differing much in style and detail, these houses are all built according to a certain general plan which shall be described later.

All this work has been done by ordinary labourers working under a contractor—a large body of men, many of whom are brought from a distance ; and they are highly paid in order to ensure that the work shall be of the best.

A great deal of complicated machinery is required for the work of the colony, and in their early days men from without are employed to manage this and to instruct the colonists in its use; but in a few years the colonists learn how to make and repair everything that is necessary for their well-being, and so they are able to dispense with outside help. Even within the first generation the colony becomes self-supporting, and after this no labour is imported from outside. A vast amount of money is expended in establishing the colony and bringing it into working order, but when once it is firmly established it is entirely self-supporting and independent of the outer world. The community does not, however, lose touch with the rest of the world, for it always takes care to acquaint itself with all new discoveries and inventions, and with any improvements in machinery.

CHILDREN OF THE MANU

The principal investigations which we made, however, concern a period about one hundred and fifty years later than this, when the community has already enormously increased, and numbers somewhere about a hundred thousand people, all of them direct physical descendants of the Manu, with the exception of a few who have been admitted from the outer world under conditions which shall presently be described. It at first seemed to us improbable that the descendants of one man could in that period amount to so large a number; but such cursory examination as could be made of the intervening period showed that all this had happened quite naturally.

When the Manu sees fit to marry, certain of His pupils selected by Him stand ready voluntarily to resign their old bodies as soon as He is able to provide them with new ones. He has twelve children in all; it is noteworthy that He arranges that each shall be born under a special influence—as astrologers would say, one under each sign of the Zodiac. All these children grow up in due course, and marry selected children of other members of the community.

Every precaution is taken to supply perfectly healthy and suitable surroundings, so that there is no infant mortality, and what we should call quite large families are the rule. At a period of fifty years after the founding of the community one hundred and four grandchildren of the Manu are already living. At eighty years from the commencement, the number of descendants is too great to be readily counted; but taking at random ten out of the hundred and four grandchildren, we find that those ten, by that time, have between them ninety-five children, which gives us a rough estimate of one thousand direct descendants in that generation, not including the original twelve children and one hundred and and four grandchildren. Moving on another quarter of a century—that is to say one hundred and five years from the original founding of the community, we find fully ten thousand direct descendants, and it then becomes clear that in the course of the next forty-five years there is not the slightest difficulty in accounting for fully one hundred thousand.

GOVERNMENT

It is now necessary to describe the government and the general conditions of our

community, to see what are its methods of
education and of worship, and its relation with
the outer world. This last appears entirely
amicable; the community pays some quite
nominal tax for its land to the general government of the country, and in return it is left
almost entirely alone, since it makes its own
roads and requires no services of any sort
from the outside government.

It is popularly regarded with great respect;
its members are considered as very good and
earnest people, though unnecessarily ascetic
in certain ways. Visitors from outside sometimes come in parties, just as tourists might in
the twentieth century, to admire the Temples
and other buildings. They are not in any way
hindered, though they are not in any way
encouraged. The comment of the visitors
generally seems to be along the lines : " Well,
it is all very beautiful and interesting, yet I
should not like to have to live as they do ! "

As the members have been separated from
the outside world for a century and a half,
old family connections have fallen into the
background. In a few cases such relationships
are still remembered, and occasionally visits

are interchanged. There is no restriction whatever upon this; a member of the colony may go and visit a friend outside of it, or may invite a friend quite freely to come and stay with him. The only rule with regard to these matters is that intermarriage between those within the community and those outside is strictly forbidden. Even such visits as have been described are infrequent, for the whole thought of the community is so entirely one-pointed that persons from the outside world are not likely to find its daily life interesting to them.

THE SPIRIT OF THE NEW RACE

For the one great dominant fact about this community is the spirit which pervades it. Every member of it knows that he is there for a definite purpose, of which he never for a moment loses sight. All have vowed themselves to the service of the Manu for the promotion of the progress of the new Race. All of them definitely mean business; every man has the fullest possible confidence in the wisdom of the Manu, and would never think of disputing any regulation which He made. We must remember that these people are a selection of a selection. During the intervening centuries many thousands have been attracted by Theosophy, and out of these the most earnest and the most thoroughly permeated by these ideas have been chosen.

Most of them have recently taken a number of rapid incarnations, bringing through to a large extent their memory, and in all of those incarnations they have known that their lives in the new Race would have to be entirely lives of self-sacrifice for the sake of that Race. They have therefore trained themselves in the putting aside of all personal desires, and there is consequently an exceedingly strong public opinion among them in favour of unselfishness, so that anything like even the slightest manifestation of personality would be considered as a shame and a disgrace.

The idea is strongly engrained that in this selection a glorious opportunity has been offered to them, and that to prove themselves unworthy of it, and in consequence to leave the community for the outer world, would be an indelible stain upon their honour.

In addition, the praise of the Manu goes to those who make advancement, who can suggest anything new and useful and assist in the development of the community, and not to anyone who does anything in the least personal. The existence among them of this great force of public opinion practically obviates the necessity of laws in the ordinary sense of the word. The whole community may not inaptly be compared to an army going into battle; if there are any private differences between individual soldiers, for the moment all these are lost in the one thought of perfect co-operation for the purpose of defeating the enemy. If any sort of difference of opinion arises between two members of the community, it is immediately submitted either to the Manu, or to the nearest member of His Council, and no one thinks of disputing the decision which is given.

The Manu and His Council

It will be seen therefore that government in the ordinary sense of the term scarcely exists in this community. The Manu's ruling is undisputed, and He gathers round Him a Council of about a dozen of the most highly developed of His pupils, some of them already Adepts at the Asekha level, who are also the Heads of departments in the management of affairs, and are constantly making new experiments with a view to increasing the welfare and efficiency of the Race. All members of the Council are sufficiently developed to function freely on all the lower planes, at least up to the level of the causal body; consequently we may think of them as practically in perpetual session—as constantly consulting, even in the very act of administration.

Anything in the nature either of courts of law or a police force does not exist, nor are such things required; for there is naturally no criminality nor violence amongst a body of people so entirely devoted to one object. Clearly, if it were conceivable that any member of the community could offend against the spirit of it, the only punishment which would or could be meted out to him would be expulsion from it; but as that would be to him the end of all his hopes, the utter failure of aspirations cherished through many lives, it is not to be supposed that anyone would run the slightest risk of it.

In thinking of the general temper of the people it must also be borne in mind that some degree of psychical perception is practically universal, and that in the case of many it is already quite highly developed; so that all can see for themselves something of the working of the forces with which they have to deal, and the enormously greater advancement of the Manu, the Chief Priest and Their Council is obvious as a definite and indubitable fact, so that all have before their eyes the strongest of reasons for accepting their decisions. In ordinary physical life, even when men have perfect confidence in the wisdom and good will of a ruler, there still remains the doubt that that ruler may be misinformed on certain points, and that for that reason his decisions may not always be in accordance with abstract justice.

Here, however, no shadow of such a doubt is possible, since by daily experience it is thoroughly well known that the Manu is practically omniscient as far as the community is concerned, and that it is therefore impossible that any circumstances can escape His observation. Even if His judgment upon any case should be different from what was expected, it would be fully understood by His people that that was not because any circumstances affecting it were unknown to Him, but rather because He was taking into account circumstances unknown to *them*.

Thus we see that the two types of people which are perpetually causing trouble in ordinary life do not exist in this community —those who intentionally break laws with the object of gaining something for themselves, and those others who cause disturbance because they fancy themselves wronged or misunderstood. The first class cannot exist here, because only those are admitted to the community who leave self behind and entirely devote themselves to its good; the second class cannot exist here because it is clear to all of them that misunderstanding or injustice is an impossibility. Under conditions such as these the problem of government becomes easy.

CHAPTER III

RELIGION AND THE TEMPLES

THIS practical absence of all regulations gives
to the whole place an air of remarkable
freedom, although at the same time the atmosphere of one-pointedness impresses itself upon
us very forcibly. Men are of many different
types, and are moving along lines of development through intellect, devotion and action ;
but all alike recognize that the Manu knows
thoroughly well what He is doing, and that all
these different ways are only so many methods
of serving Him—that whatever development
comes to one comes to him not for himself, but
for the Race, that it may be handed on to his
children. There are no longer different religions in our sense of the word, though the one
teaching is given in different typical forms.
The subject of religious worship is, however,
of such great importance that we will now
devote a special section to its consideration,

following this up with the new methods of education, and the particulars of the personal, social, and corporate life of the community.

THEOSOPHY IN THE COMMUNITY

Since the two Masters who founded the Theosophical Society are also the leaders of this community, it is quite natural that the religious opinion current there should be what we now call Theosophy. All that we now hold—all that is known in the innermost circles of our Esoteric Section—is the common faith of the community, and many points on which as yet our own knowledge is only rudimentary are thoroughly grasped and understood in detail. The outline of our Theosophy is no longer a matter of discussion but of certainty, and the facts of the life after death and the existence and nature of the higher worlds are matters of experimental knowledge for nearly all members of the colony.

Here, as in our own time, different branches of the study attract different people; some think chiefly of the higher philosophy and metaphysics, while the majority prefer to express their religious feelings along some of the lines provided for them in the different Temples. A strong vein of practicality runs through all their thinking, and we should not go far wrong in saying that the religion of this community is to do what it is told. There is no sort of divorcement between science and religion, because both alike are bent entirely to the one object, and exist only for the sake of the State. Men no longer worship various manifestations, since all possess accurate knowledge as to the existence of the Solar Deity. It is still the custom with many to make a salutation to the Sun as he rises, but all are fully aware that he is to be regarded as a centre in the body of the Deity.

THE DEVAS

One prominent feature of the religious life is the extent to which the Devas take part in it. Many religions of the twentieth century spoke of a Golden Age in the past in which Angels or Deities walked freely among men, but this happy state of things had then ceased

because of the grossness of that stage
of evolution. As regards our community
this has again been realized, for great
Devas habitually come among the people
and bring to them many new possibilities
of development, each drawing to himself
those cognate to his own nature. This
should not surprise us, for even in the
twentieth century much help was being given
by Devas to those who were able to receive it.

Such opportunities of learning, such
avenues of advancement, were not then open
to the majority, but this was not because of
the unwillingness of the Devas, but because of
man's backwardness in evolution. We were
then much in the position of children in a
primary class in this world-school. The great
professors from the universities sometimes
came to our school to instruct the advanced
students, and we sometimes saw them pass at
a distance; but their ministrations were as
yet of no direct use to us simply because we
were not at the age or stage of development at
which we could make any use of them. The
classes were being held. The teachers were
there, quite at our disposal as soon as we grew

3

old enough. Our community *has* grown old enough, and therefore it is reaping the benefit of constant intercourse with these great beings and of frequent instruction from them.

THE TEMPLE SERVICES

These Devas are not merely making sporadic appearances, but are definitely working as part of the regular organization under the direction of the Chief Priest, who takes entire control of the religious development of the community, and of its educational department. For the outward expression of this religion we find that various classes of Temple services are provided, and that the management of these is the especial function of the Devas. Four types of these Temples were observed, and though the outline and objects of the services were the same in all, there were striking differences in form and method, which we shall now endeavour to describe.

The key-note of the Temple service is that each man, belonging as he does to a particular type, has some one avenue through which he can most easily reach the Divine, and therefore be most easily reached in turn by divine influence. In some men that channel is affection, in others devotion, in others sympathy, in yet others intellect. For these four kinds of Temples exist, and in each of them the object is to bring the prominent quality in the man into active and conscious relationship with the corresponding quality in the LOGOS of which it is a manifestation, for in that way the man himself can most easily be uplifted and helped.

Thereby he can be raised for a time to a level of spirituality and power far beyond anything that is normally possible for him; and every such effort of spiritual elevation makes the next similar effort easier for him, and also raises slightly his normal level. Every service which a man attends is intended to have a definite and calculated effect upon him, and the services for a year or series of years are carefully ordered with a view to the average development of the congregation, and with the idea of carrying its members upward to a certain point. It is in this work that the co-operation of the Deva is so valuable, since he acts as a true priest and intermediary between the people and the LOGOS, receiving, gathering together and forwarding their streams of aspirational force, and distributing, applying and bringing down to their level the floods of divine influence which come as a response from on high.

THE CRIMSON TEMPLE

The first Temple entered for the purposes of examination was one of those which the Deva originally showed in his pictures—one of those where progress is principally made through affection, a great characteristic of the services of which is the splendid flood of colour which accompanies them, and is in fact their principal expression. Imagine a magnificent circular building somewhat resembling a cathedral, yet of no order of architecture at present known to us, and much more open to the outer air than it is possible for any cathedral to be in ordinary European climates. Imagine it filled with a reverent congregation, and the Deva-priest standing in the centre before them, on the apex of a kind of pyramidal or conical erection of filigree work, so that he is equally visible from every part of the great building.

It is noteworthy that every worshipper as he enters takes his seat on the pavement quietly and reverently, and then closes his eyes and passes before his mental vision a succession of sheets or clouds of colour, such as sometimes pass before one's eyes in the darkness just before falling asleep. Each person has an order of his own for these colours, and they are evidently to some extent a personal expression of him. This seems to be of the nature of the preliminary prayer on entering a church of the twentieth century, and is intended to calm the man, to collect his thoughts, if they have been wandering, and to attune him to the surrounding atmosphere and the purpose which it subserves. When the service commences the Deva materializes on the apex of his pyramid, assuming for the occasion a magnificent and glorified human form, and wearing in these particular Temples flowing vestments of rich crimson (the colour varies with the type of Temple, as will presently be seen).

His first action is to cause a flashing-out above his head of a band of brilliant colours somewhat resembling a solar spectrum, save that on different occasions the colours are in different order and vary in their proportions. It is practically impossible to describe this band of colours with accuracy, for it is much more than a mere spectrum : it is a picture, yet not a picture; it has within it geometrical forms, yet we have at present no means by which it can be drawn or represented, for it is in more dimensions than are known to our senses as they are now constituted.

This band is the key-note or text of that particular service, indicating to those who understand it the exact object which it is intended to attain, and the direction in which their affection and aspiration must be outpoured. It is a thought expressed in the colour-language of the Devas, and is intelligible as such to all the congregation. It is materially visible on the physical plane, as well as on the astral and mental, for although the majority of the congregation are likely to possess at least astral sight, there may still be some for whom such sight is only occasional.

Each person present now attempts to imitate this text or key-note, forming by the power of his will in the air in front of himself a smaller band of colours as nearly like it as he can. Some succeed far better than others, so that each such attempt expresses not only the subject indicated by the Deva but also the character of the man who makes it. Some are able to make this so definitely that it is visible on the physical plane, while others can make it only at astral and mental levels. Some of those who produce the most brilliant and successful imitations of the form made by the Deva do not bring it down to the physical plane.

The Deva, holding out his arms over the people, now pours out through this colour-form a wonderful stream of influence upon them—a stream which reaches them through their own corresponding colour-forms and uplifts them precisely in the proportion in which they have been successful in making their colour-forms resemble that of the Deva. The influence is not that of the Deva-priest alone, for above and altogether beyond him, and apart from the Temple or the material world, stands a ring of higher Devas for whose forces he acts as a channel.

The astral effect of the outpouring is remarkable. A sea of pale crimson light suffuses the vast aura of the Deva and spreads out in great waves over the congregation, thus acting upon them and stirring their emotions into greater activity. Each of them shoots up into the rose-coloured sea his own particular form, but beautiful though that is, it is naturally of a lower order than that of the Deva, individually coarser and less brilliant than the totality of brilliancy in which it flashes forth, and so we have a curious and beautiful effect of deep crimson flames piercing a rose-coloured sea—as one might imagine volcanic flames shooting up in front of a gorgeous sunset.

To understand to some extent how this activity of sympathetic vibration is brought about we must realize that the aura of a Deva is far more extensive than that of a human being, and it is also far more flexible. The feeling which in an ordinary man expresses itself in a smile of greeting, in a Deva causes a sudden expansion and brightening of the aura, and manifests not only in colour but also in musical sound. A greeting from one Deva to another is a splendid chord of music, or rather an arpeggio; a conversation between two Devas is like a fugue; an oration delivered by one of them is a splendid oratorio.

A Rūpadeva of ordinary development has frequently an aura of many hundred yards in diameter, and when anything interests him or excites his enthusiasm it instantly increases enormously. Our Deva-priest therefore is including the whole of his congregation within his aura, and is consequently able to act upon them in a most intimate manner— from within as well as from without. Our readers may perhaps picture to themselves this aura, if they recollect that of the Arhat in *Man Visible and Invisible*; but they must think of it as less fixed and more fluidic, more fiery and sparkling—as consisting almost entirely of pulsating fiery rays, which yet give much the same general effect of arrangement of colour. It is as though those spheres of colour remain, but are formed of fiery rays which are ever flowing outward, yet as they pass through each section of the radius they take upon themselves its colour.

THE LINKS WITH THE LOGOS

This first outpouring of influence upon the people has the effect of bringing each person up to his highest level, and evoking from him the noblest affection of which he is capable. When the Deva sees that all are tuned to the proper key, he reverses the current of his force, he concentrates and defines his aura into a smaller spherical form, out of the top of which rises a huge column reaching upwards. Instead of extending his arms over the people he raises them above his head, and at that signal every man in the congregation sends towards the Deva-priest the utmost wealth of his affection and aspiration—pours himself out in worship and love at the feet of the Deity. The Deva draws all those fiery streams into himself, and pours them upward in one vast fountain of many-coloured flame, which expands as it rises and is caught by the circle of waiting Devas, who pass it through themselves and, transmuting it, converge it, like rays refracted through a lens, until it reaches the great chief Deva of their Ray, the mighty potentate who looks upon the very LOGOS Himself, and represents that Ray in relation to Him.

That great Chieftain is collecting similar streams from all parts of his world, and he weaves these many streams into one great rope which binds the earth to the Feet of its GOD; he combines these many streams into the one great river which flows round those Feet, and brings our petal of the lotus close to the heart of the flower. And He answers. In the light of the LOGOS Himself shines forth for a moment a yet greater brilliancy; back to the great Deva Chieftain flashes that instant recognition; through him on the waiting ring below flows down that flood of power; and as through them it touches the Deva-priest expectant on his pinnacle, once more he lowers his arms and spreads them out above his people in benediction. A flood of colours gorgeous beyond all description fills the whole vast cathedral; torrents as of liquid fire, yet delicate as the hues of an Egyptian sunset, are bathing every one in their effulgence; and out of all this glory each one takes to himself that which he is able to take, that which the stage of his development enables him to assimilate.

All the vehicles of each man present are vivified into their highest activity by this stupendous down-rush of divine power, and for the moment each realizes to his fullest capacity what the life of God really means, and how in each it must express itself as love for his fellow-man. This is a far fuller and more personal benediction than that poured out at the beginning of the service, for here is something exactly fitted to each man, strengthening him in his weakness and yet at the same time developing to its highest possibility all that is best in him, giving him not only a tremendous and transcendent experience at the time, but also a memory which shall be for him as a radiant and glowing light for many a day to come. This is the daily service—the daily religious practice of those who belong to this Ray of affection.

Nor does the good influence of this service affect only those who are present; its radiations extend over a large district, and purify the astral and mental atmospheres. The effect is distinctly perceptible to any moderately sensitive person even two or three miles from the Temple. Each such service also sends out a huge eruption of rose-coloured thought-forms which bombard the surrounding country with thoughts of love, so that the whole atmosphere is full of it. In the Temple itself a vast crimson vortex is set up which is largely permanent, so that anyone entering the Temple immediately feels its influence, and this also keeps up a steady radiation upon the surrounding district. In addition to this each man as he goes home from the service is himself a centre of force of no mean order, and when he reaches his home the radiations which pour from him are strongly perceptible to any neighbours who have not been able to attend the service.

THE SERMON

Sometimes, in addition to this, or perhaps as a service apart from this, the Deva delivers what may be described as a kind of colour-sermon, taking up that colour-form which we have mentioned as the key-note or text for the day, explaining it to his people by an unfolding process, and mostly without spoken words, and perhaps causing it to pass through a series of mutations intended to convey to them instruction of various kinds. One exceedingly vivid and striking colour-sermon of this nature was intended to show the effect of love upon the various qualities in others with which it comes into contact. The black clouds of malice, the scarlet of anger, the dirty green of deceit, the hard brown-grey of selfishness, the brownish-green of jealousy, and the heavy dull-grey of depression, were all in turn subjected to the glowing crimson fire of love. The stages through which they pass were shown, and it was made clear that in the end none of them could resist its force, and all of them at last melted into it and were consumed.

INCENSE

Though colour is in every way the principal feature in this service which we have described, the Deva does not disdain to avail himself of

the channels of other senses than that of sight.
All through his service, and even before it
began, incense has been kept burning in
swinging censers underneath his golden
pyramid, where stand two boys to attend to it.
The kind of incense burnt varies with the
different parts of the service. The people
are far more sensitive to perfumes than
we of earlier centuries; they are able to
distinguish accurately all the different kinds
of incense, and they know exactly what each
kind means and for what purpose it is used.
The number of pleasant odours available
in this way is much larger than in the
present day, and they have discovered
some method of making them more volatile,
so that they penetrate instantly through every
part of the building. This acts upon the
etheric body somewhat as the colours do upon
the astral, and bears its part in bringing all
the vehicles of the man rapidly into harmony.
These people possess a good deal of new information as to the effect of odours upon
certain parts of the brain, as we shall see more
fully when we come to deal with the educational processes.

Sound

Naturally every change of colour is accompanied by its appropriate sound, and though this is a subordinate feature in the colour-temple which we have described, it is yet by no means without its effect. We shall now, however, attempt to describe a somewhat similar service in a Temple where music is the predominant feature, and colour comes only to assist its effect, precisely as sound has assisted colour in the Temple of affection. In common parlance, these Temples in which progress is made principally by the development of affection are called 'crimson Temples'—first because everyone knows that crimson is the colour in the aura which indicates affection, and therefore that is the prevailing colour of all the splendid outpourings which take place in it; and secondly, because in recognition of the same fact all the graceful lines of the architecture are indicated by lines of crimson, and there are even some Temples entirely of that hue.

The majority of these Temples are built of a stone of a beautiful pale grey with a polished surface much like that of marble, and when this is the case only the external decorations are of the colour which indicates the nature of the services performed within. Sometimes, however, the Temples of affection are built entirely of stone of a lovely pale rose-colour, which stands out with marvellous beauty against the vivid green of the trees with which they are always surrounded. The Temples in which music is the dominant factor are similarly known as 'blue Temples,' because, since their principal object is the arousing of the highest possible devotion, blue is the colour most prominent in connection with their services, and consequently the colour adopted for both exterior and interior decoration.

THE BLUE TEMPLE

The general outline of the services in one of the blue Temples closely resembles that which we have already described, except that in their case sound takes the place of colour as the principal agent. Just as the endeavour in the colour-Temple was to stimulate the love

4

in man by bringing it consciously into relation with the divine love, so in this Temple the object is to promote the evolution of the man through the quality of devotion, which by the use of music is enormously uplifted and intensified and brought into direct relation with the LOGOS who is its object. Just as in the crimson Temple there exists a permanent vortex of the highest and noblest affection, so in this music-Temple there exists a similar atmosphere of unselfish devotion which instantly affects every one who enters it.

Into this atmosphere come the members of the congregation, each bringing in his hand a curious musical instrument, unlike any formerly known on earth. It is not a violin; it is perhaps rather of the nature of a small circular harp with strings of some shining metal. But this strange instrument has many remarkable properties. It is in fact much more than a mere instrument; it is specially magnetized for its owner, and no other person must use it. It is tuned to the owner; it is an expression of the owner—a funnel through which he can be reached on this physical plane. He plays upon it, and yet at the same time he

himself is affected in doing so. He gives out
and receives vibrations through it.

THE DEVOTIONAL SERVICE

When the worshipper enters the Temple,
he calls up before his mind a succession of
beautiful sounds—a piece of music which
fulfils for him the same office as the series of
colours which pass before the eyes of the man
in the colour-Temple at the same stage of the
proceedings. When the Deva materializes he
also takes up an instrument of similar nature,
and he commences the service by striking
upon it a chord (or rather an arpeggio) which
fulfils the function of the keynote in colour
which is used in the other Temple. The
effect of this chord is most striking. His
instrument is but a small one and apparently
of no great power, though wonderfully sweet
in tone ; but as he strikes it, the chord seems
to be taken up in the air around him as though
it were repeated by a thousand invisible
musicians, so that it resounds through the
great dome of the Temple and pours out in a
flood of harmony, a sea of rushing sound, over
the entire congregation.

Each member of the congregation now touches his own instrument, very softly at first, but gradually swelling out into a greater volume, until everyone is taking part in this wonderful symphony. Thus, as in the colour-Temple, every member is brought into harmony with the principal idea which the Deva wishes to emphasize at this service, and in this case, as in the other, a benediction is poured over the people which raises each to the highest level possible for him, and draws from him an eager response, which shows itself both in sound and in colour.

Here also incense is being used, and it varies at different points of the service, much as in the other case. Then when the congregation is thoroughly tuned, each man begins definitely to play. All are clearly taking recognized parts, although it does not seem that this has been arranged or rehearsed beforehand. As soon as this stage is in full operation the Deva-priest draws in his aura, and begins to pour his sound inwards instead of out over the people. Each man is putting his very life into his playing, and definitely aiming at the Deva, so that through him it may rise.

The effect on the higher emotions of the people is most remarkable, and the living aspiration and devotion of the congregation is poured upwards in a mighty stream through the officiating Deva to a great circle of Devas above, who, as before, draw it into themselves, transmuting it to an altogether higher level, and send it forward in a still mightier stream towards the great Deva at the head of their Ray. Upon him converge thousands of such streams from all the devotion of the earth, and he in his turn gathers all these together and weaves them into one, which, as he sends it upwards, links him with the solar LOGOS Himself.

In it he is bearing his share in a concert which comes from all the worlds of the system, and these streams from all the worlds make somehow the mighty twelve-stringed lyre upon which the LOGOS Himself plays as He sits upon the Lotus of His system. It is impossible to put this into words; but the writer has seen it, and knows that it is true. He hears, He responds, and He Himself plays upon His system. Thus for the first time we have one brief glimpse of the stupendous life which He lives among the other LOGOI who are His peers; but thought fails before this glory; our minds are inadequate to comprehend it. At least it is clear that the great music-Devas, taken in their totality, represent music to the LOGOS, and He expresses Himself through them in music to His worlds.

THE BENEDICTION

Then comes the response—a downpouring flood of ordered sound too tremendous to be described, flowing back through the Chieftain of the Ray to the circle of Devas below, and from them to the Deva-priest in the Temple, transmuted at each stage to lower levels, so that at last it pours out through the officiant in the Temple in a form in which it may be assimilated by his congregation—a great ocean of soft, sweet, swelling sound, an outburst of celestial music which surrounds, enwraps, overwhelms them, and yet pours into them through their own instruments vibrations so living, so uplifting, that their higher bodies are brought into action and their consciousness is raised to levels which in their outer life it could not even approach. Each man holds out his instrument in front of him, and it is through that that this marvellous effect is produced upon him. It seems as though from the great symphony each instrument selected the chords appropriate to itself—that is to say, to the owner whose expression it is. Yet each harp somehow not only selects and responds, but also calls into existence far more than its own volume of sound.

The whole atmosphere is surcharged by the Gandharvas, or music-Devas, so that veritably every sound is multiplied, and for every single tone is produced a great chord of overtones and undertones, all of unearthly sweetness and beauty. This benedictory response from on high is an utterly amazing experience, but words completely fail when we endeavour to find expression for it. It must be seen and heard and felt before it can in any way be understood.

This magnificent final swell goes sounding home with the people, as it were; it lives inside them still even though the service is

over, and often the member will try to
reproduce it in a minor degree in a kind of
little private service at home. In this Temple
also there may be what corresponds to a
sermon, but in this case it is delivered by the
Deva through his instrument and received by
the people through theirs. It is clear that it
is not the same to all—that some gather more
and some less of the meaning of the Deva and
of the effect which he intends to produce.

INTELLECT

All the effects which are produced in the
crimson Temple through affection by the
gorgeous seas of colour are attained here
through devotion by this marvellous use of
music. It is clear that in both cases the action
is primarily on the intuitional and emotional
bodies of the people—on the intuitional directly,
in those who have developed it to the responsive
stage, and on the intuitional through the
emotional for others who are somewhat less
advanced. The intellect is touched only by
reflection from these planes, whereas in the
next variety of Temple to be described this

action is reversed, for the stimulation is brought to bear directly upon the intellect, and it is only through and by means of that that the intuitional is presently to be awakened. Eventual results are no doubt the same, but the order of procedure is different.

THE YELLOW TEMPLE

If we think of the men of the crimson Temple as developing through colour, and those of the blue as utilizing sound, we might perhaps put form as the vehicle principally employed in the yellow Temple—for naturally yellow is the colour of the Temple especially devoted to intellectual development, since it is in that way that it symbolizes itself in the various vehicles of man.

Once more the architecture and the internal structure of the Temple are the same, except that all decorations and outlinings are in yellow instead of blue or crimson. The general scheme of the service, too, is identical—the text or keynote first, which brings all into union, then the aspiration or prayer or effort of the people, which calls down the response from the Logos.

The form of instruction which, for want of a better name, I have called the sermon also has its part in all the services. All alike use incense, though the difference between the kind used in this yellow Temple and that of the blue and the crimson is noticeable. The vortex in this case stimulates intellectual activity, so that merely to enter the Temple makes a man feel more keenly alive mentally, better able to understand and to appreciate.

These people do not bring with them any physical instruments, and instead of passing before their eyes a succession of clouds of colour, they begin, as soon as they take their seats, to visualise certain mental forms. Each man has his own form, which is clearly intended to be an expression of himself, just as was the physical instrument of the musician, or the special colour-scheme of the worshipper in the Temple of affection. These forms are all different, and many of them distinctly imply the power to visualize in the physical brain some of the simpler four-dimensional figures.

Naturally the power of visualization differs; so some people are able to make their figures much more complete and definite than others. But, curiously, the indefiniteness seems to show itself at both ends of the scale. The less educated of the thinkers—those who are as yet only learning how to think—often make forms which are not clearly cut, or even if at first they are able to make them clear they are not able to maintain them so, and they constantly slip into indefiniteness. They do not actually materialize them, but they do form them strongly in mental matter, and almost all of them, even at quite an early stage, seem to be able to do this.

The forms are evidently at first prescribed for them, and they are told to hold them rather as a means than as an object of contemplation. They are clearly intended to be each an expression of its creator, whose further progress will involve modifications of the form, though these do not change it essentially. He is intended to think through it and to receive vibrations through it, just as the musical man received them through his instrument, or the member of the colour congregation through his colour-form. With the more intelligent persons the form becomes more definite and more complicated ; but with some of the most definite of all it is again taking on an appearance suggesting indefiniteness, because it is beginning to be so much upon a still higher plane—because it is taking on more and more of the dimensions, and is becoming so living that it cannot be kept still.

THE INTELLECTUAL STIMULUS

When the Deva appears he also makes a form—not a form which is an expression of himself, but, as in the other Temples, one which is to be the keynote of the service, which defines the special object at which on this occasion he is aiming. His congregation then project themselves into their forms, and try through those to respond to his form and to understand it. Sometimes it is a changing form—one which unfolds or unveils itself in a number of successive movements. Along with the formation of this, and through it, the Deva-priest pours out upon them a great flood of yellow light which applies intense stimulus to their intellectual faculties along the particular line which he is indicating.

He is acting strongly upon both their causal and mental bodies, but very little comparatively on the emotional or the intuitional. Some who have not normally the consciousness of the mental body have it awakened in them by this process, so that for the first time they can use it quite freely and see clearly by its means. In others, who have it not normally, it awakens the power of four-dimensional sight for the first time ; in others less advanced it only makes them see things a little more clearly, and comprehend temporarily ideas which are usually too metaphysical for them.

INTELLECTUAL FEELING

The mental effort is not entirely unaccompanied by feeling, for there is at least an intense delight in reaching upwards, though even that very delight is felt almost exclusively through the mental body. They all pour their thoughts through their forms into the

Deva-priest, as before, and they offer up these individual contributions as a kind of sacrifice to the LOGOS of the best that they have to give. Into him and through him they give themselves in surrender to the burning Light above ; they merge themselves, throw themselves, into him. It is the white heat of intellectuality raised to its highest power. As in the other Temples, the Deva-priest synthesizes all the different forms which are sent to him, and blends together all the streams of force, before forwarding it to the circle above him, which this time consists of that special class which for the present we will call the yellow Devas—those who are developing intellect, and revel in assisting and guiding it in man.

As before, they absorb the force, but only to send it out again at a higher level and enormously increased in quantity to the great Chieftain who is the head of their Ray, and a kind of centre for the exchange of forces. The intellect aspect of the LOGOS plays upon him and through him from above, while all human intellect reaches up to him and through him from below. He receives and forwards the contribution from the Temple, and in turn he opens the flood-gates of divine intelligence which, lowered through many stages on the way, pours out upon the waiting people and raises them out of their every-day selves into what they will be in the future.

The temporary effect of such a downpouring is almost incalculable. All egos present are brought into vigorous activity, and the consciousness in the causal body is brought into action in all of those in whom it is as yet in any way possible. In others it means merely greatly increased mental activity; some are so lifted out of themselves that they actually leave the body, and others pass into a kind of Samādhi, because the consciousness is drawn up into a vehicle which is not yet sufficiently developed to be able to express it.

The response from above is not merely a stimulation. It contains also a vast mass of forms—it would seem all possible forms along whatever is the special line of the day. These forms also are assimilated by such of the congregation as can utilize them, and it is noteworthy that the same form means much more to some people than to others. For example, a form which conveys some interesting detail of physical evolution to one man may to another represent a whole vast stage of cosmic development.

For many people it is as though they were seeing in visible form the Stanzas of Dzyān. All are trying to think on the same line, yet they do it in different ways, and consequently they attract to themselves different forms out of the vast ordered system which is at their disposal. Each man draws out of this multitude that which is most suited to him. Some people, for example, are simply acquiring new lights on the subject, substituting for their own thought-form another which is in reality in no way superior to it, but simply another side of the question.

Men are evidently raised into the intuitional consciousness along these lines. By intense thinking, by comprehension of the converging streams, they attain first an intellectual grasp of the constitution of the universe, and then by intense pressure upwards they realize it and break through. It usually comes with a rush and almost overwhelms the man—all the more so as along his line he has had little

practice before in understanding the feelings
of humanity. From his intellectual point of
view he has been philosophically examining
and dissecting people, as though they were
plants under a microscope ; and now, in a
moment, it is borne in upon him that all these
also are divine as himself, that all these are
full of their own feelings and emotions, under-
standings and misunderstandings, that these are
more than brothers, since they are actually
within himself and not without. This is a
great shock for the man to whom it comes,
and he needs time to readjust himself and to
develop some other qualities which he has been
hitherto to some extent neglecting. The
service ends much as the others did, and each
man's mental form is permanently somewhat
the better for the exercise through which he
has passed.

MENTAL MAGIC

Here also we have the form of instruction
which we have called the sermon, and in this
case it is usually an exposition of the changes
which take place in a certain form or set of

5

forms. In this case the Deva occasionally makes use of spoken words, though only few of them. It is as though he were showing them changing magic-lantern pictures, and naming them as they pass before them. He materializes strongly and clearly the special thought-form which he is showing them, and each member of the congregation tries to copy it in his own mental matter.

In one case which is observed, that which is described is the transference of forms from plane to plane—a kind of mental magic which shows how one thought can be changed into another. On the lower mental plane he shows how a selfish thought may become unselfish. None of his people are crudely selfish, or they would not be in the community; but there may still remain subtle forms of self-centred thought. There is a certain danger also of intellectual pride, and it is shown how this can be transmuted into worship of the wisdom of the LOGOS.

In other cases most interesting metamorphoses are shown—forms changing into one another by turning inside out like a glove. In this way, for example, a dodecahedron becomes an icosahedron. Not only are these changes shown, but also their inner meaning on all the different planes is explained, and here also it is interesting to see the unfoldment of the successive esoteric meanings and to notice how some members of the congregation stop at one of these, feeling it to the highest possible degree, and well satisfied with themselves for being able to see it, while others go on one, two or more stages beyond them, further into the real heart of the meaning. What is applied only as a transmutation of their own thoughts by the majority of the congregation may be to the few who have gone further a translation of cosmic force from one plane to another. Such a sermon is a veritable training in mental intensity and activity, and it needs a closely sustained attention to follow it.

In all these Temples alike a great point is made of the training of the will which is necessary in order to keep the attention focused upon all the different parts of their variations in the pictures, the music, or the thought-forms. All this is shown most prominently by the intense glow of the causal bodies, but it reacts upon the mental vehicles and even upon the physical brain, which appears on the whole to be distinctly larger among these pioneers of the sixth Root Race than with men of the fifth. It used to be thought by many that much study and intellectual development tended greatly to atrophy or destroy the power of visualization, but that is not at all the case with the devotees of the yellow Temple. Perhaps the difference may be that in the old days study was so largely a study of mere words, whereas in the case of all these people they have for many lives been devoting themselves also to meditation, which necessarily involves the constant practice of visualization in a high degree.

THE GREEN TEMPLE

Yet one more type of Temple remains to be described—a type which is decorated in a lovely pale green, because the thought-forms generated in it are of precisely that colour. Of the Temples already mentioned the crimson and the blue seem to have many points in common, and a similar link seems to join the yellow and the green. One might perhaps say that the blue and the crimson correspond to two types of what in India is called Bhakti-yoga; in that case the yellow Temple might be thought of as offering us the Jñāna-yoga, and the green Temple the Karma-yoga; or in English we might characterize them as the Temples of affection, devotion, intellect and action respectively.

The congregation of the green Temple works also chiefly on the mental plane, but its particular line is the translating of thought into action—to get things done. It is part of its regular service to send out intentionally arranged thought-currents, primarily towards its own community, but also through them to the world at large. In the other Temples too they think of the outside world, for they include it in their thoughts of love and devotion or treat it intellectually; but the idea of these people of the green Temple is action with regard to everything, and they consider that they have not surely grasped an idea until they have translated it into action.

The people of the yellow Temple, on the other hand, take the same idea quite differently, and consider it perfectly possible to have the fullest comprehension without action. But the devotees of this green Temple cannot feel that they are really fulfilling their place in the world unless they are constantly in active motion. A thought-form to them is not an effective thought-form unless it contains some of their typical green—because, as they say, it is lacking in sympathy—so that all their forces express themselves in action, action, action, and in action is their happiness, and through the self-sacrifice in the action they attain.

They have powerful and concentrated plans in their minds, and in some cases it is noticed that many of them combine to think out one plan and to have the thing done. They are careful to accumulate much knowledge about whatever subject they take up as a speciality. Often each one takes some area in the world into which he pours his thought-forms for a certain object. One, for example, will take up education in Greenland, or social reform in Kamschatka. They are naturally dealing with all sorts of out-of-the-way places like these, because by this time everything conceivable has already been done in every place of which we have ever heard in ordinary life. They do not use hypnotism, however ; they do not in any way try to dominate the will of any man whom they wish to help; they simply try to impress their ideas and improvements on his brain.

THE LINE OF THE HEALING DEVAS

Once more, the general scheme of their service is like that of the others. They do not bring with them any physical instruments, but they have their mental forms just as the intellectual people have, only in this case they are always plans of activity. Each has some special plan to which he is devoting himself, though at the same time through it he is devoting himself to the LOGOS. They hold their plans and the realization of them before them, just in the same way as the other men do their thought- or colour-forms. It is noteworthy that these plans are always carried to a great height of conception.

For example, a man's plan for the organization of a backward country would include and be mainly centred in the idea of the mental and moral uplifting of its inhabitants. These devotees of the green Temple are not actually philanthropical in the old sense of the word, though their hearts are filled with sympathy with their fellow-men, which expresses itself in the most beautiful shade of their characteristic colour. Indeed, from what glimpses have been caught of the outer world it seems evident that ordinary philanthropy is quite unnecessary, because poverty has disappeared. Their schemes are all plans for helping people, or for the improvement of conditions in some way.

Suggestions of all kinds and sorts of activity find their place here, and they appeal to the active or healing Devas, the type identified by Christian Mystics with the hierarchy of the Archangel Raphael. Their Deva-priest puts before them as his text, or as the dominant idea of the service, something which will be an aspect of all their ideas and will strengthen every one of them. They try to present clearly their several schemes, and through that they gain development for themselves in trying to sympathize with and help other people. After the preliminary tuning up and the opening benediction, there comes once more the offering of their plans. The opening benediction may be thought of as bringing the sympathy of the Devas for all their schemes and the identification of the Deva-priest with each and all of them.

When the time of aspiration comes, each offers his plan as something of his own which he has to give, as his contribution, as the fruit of his brain, which he lays before the Lord, and also he has the thought that thus he throws himself and his life into his schemes as a sacrifice for the sake of the LOGOS. Once more we have the same magnificent effect, the splendid sheet and fountains, the great glowing sea of pale luminous sunset green, and among it the flames of darker green shooting up from the sympathetic thought of each member present. Just as before, all this is gathered into a focus by the Deva-priest, is sent up by him to a circle of healing Devas above, and through them to the Chieftain of their Ray, who once more presents this aspect of the world to the LOGOS.

When they thus offer themselves and their thoughts, there comes back the great flow of response, the outpouring of good-will and of blessing, which in turn illuminates the sacrifice which they have offered through the line to which each has directed himself. The great Devas seem to magnetize the man and increase his power along this and cognate lines, raising it to higher levels, even while they increase it. The response not only strengthens such thoughts of good as he already has, but also opens up to him the conception of further activities for his thoughts. It is a definite act of projection, and it is done by them in a time of silent meditation after the reception of the blessing.

There are many types among these people ; they bring different chakras or centres in the mental body into activity, and their streams of thought-force are projected some-times from one chakra and sometimes from another. In the final benediction it seems as though the LOGOS pours Himself through His Devas into them, and then again out through them to the objects of their sympathy, so that an additional transmutation of the force takes place, and the culmination of their act is to be an active agent for His action. Intense sympathy is the feeling most cultivated by these people; it is their key-note, by which they gradually rise through the mental and causal bodies to the intuitional, and there find the acme of sympathy, because there the object of sympathy is no longer outside themselves, but within.

The sermon in this case is frequently an exposition of the adaptability of various types of elemental essence to the thought-force which they require. Such a sermon is illustrated as it goes on, and the thought-forms are constructed before the congregation by the Deva and materialized for them, so that they may learn exactly the best way to produce them and the best materials of which to build them.

INDEPENDENTS

In the special lines of development of these Temples there seems a curious half-suggestion of the four lower sub-planes of the mental plane as they present themselves during the life after death, for it will be remembered that affection is the chief characteristic of one of these planes, devotion of another, action for the sake of the Deity of a third, and the clear conception of right for right's sake of the fourth. It is, however, quite evident that there is no difference in advancement between the egos who follow one line and those who follow another; all these paths are clearly equal, all alike are stairways leading from the level of ordinary humanity to the Path of Holiness which rises to the level of Adeptship. To one or other of these types belong the great majority of the people of the community, so that all these temples are daily filled with crowds of worshippers.

A few people there are who do not attend any of these services, simply because none of these are to them the most appropriate way of development. There is not, however, the slightest feeling that these few are therefore irreligious or in any way inferior to the most regular attendants. It is thoroughly recognized that there are many paths to the summit of the mountain, and that each man is absolutely at liberty to take that which seems best to him. In most cases a man selects his path and keeps to it, but it would never occur to him to blame his neighbour for selecting another, or even for declining to select any one of those provided.

Every man is trying his best in his own way to fit himself for the work that he will have to do in the future, as well as to carry out to the best of his ability the work at present before him. Nobody harbours the feeling: " I am in a better way than so-and-so," because he sees another doing differently. The habitual attendants of one Temple also quite often visit the others ; indeed, some people try them all in turn rather according to their feeling of the moment, saying to themselves: " I think I need a touch of yellow this morning to brighten up my intellect "; or: " perhaps I am becoming too metaphysical, let me try a tonic of the green Temple "; or on the other hand : " I have been straining hard lately along intellectual lines ; let me now give a turn to affection or devotion."

Congregation of the Dead

Many people also make a practice of attending the magnificent, though more elementary, services which are frequently held in the Temples, ostensibly for children; these will be described in detail when we come to the subject of education. It is interesting to observe that the peculiar nature of the Temple services of this community has evidently attracted much attention in the astral world, for large numbers of dead people make a practice of attending the services. They have discovered the participation of the Devas and the tremendous forces which are consequently playing through them, and they evidently wish to partake of the advantages. This congregation of the dead is recruited exclusively from the outside world; for in the community there are no dead, since every man, when he puts aside one physical body, promptly assumes another in order to carry on the work to which he has devoted himself.

THE MASTER OF RELIGION

The religious and educational side of the life of the community is under the direction of the Master K. H.; and He Himself makes it a point to visit all the Temples in turn, taking the place of the officiating Deva, and in doing so showing the fact that He combines within Himself in the highest possible degree all the qualities of all the types. The Devas who are doing work connected with religion and education are all marshalled under His orders. Some members of the community are being specially trained by the Devas, and it seems probable that such men will in due course pass on to the line of the Deva evolution.

CHAPTER IV

EDUCATION AND THE FAMILY

The Education of Children

As we should naturally expect, much attention is paid in this community to the education of the children. It is considered of such paramount importance that nothing which can in any way help is neglected, and all sorts of adjuncts are brought into play; colour, light, sound, form, electricity are all pressed into the service, and the Devas who take so large a part in the work avail themselves of the aid of armies of nature-spirits. It has been realized that many facts previously ignored or considered insignificant have their place and their influence in educational processes—that, for example, the surroundings most favourable for the study of mathematics are not at all necessarily the same that are best suited for music or geography.

People have learnt that different parts of the physical brain may be stimulated by different lights and colours—that for certain subjects an atmosphere slightly charged with electricity is useful, while for others it is positively detrimental. In the corner of every class-room, therefore, there stands a variant upon an electrical machine, by means of which the surrounding conditions can be changed at will. Some rooms are hung with yellow, decorated exclusively with yellow flowers, and permeated with yellow light. In others, on the contrary, blue, red, violet, green or white predominates. Various perfumes are also found to have a stimulating effect, and these also are employed according to a regular system.

Perhaps the most important innovation is the work of the nature-spirits, who take a keen delight in executing the tasks committed to them, and enjoy helping and stimulating the children much as gardeners might delight in the production of especially fine plants. Among other things they take up all the appropriate influences of light and colour, sound and electricity, and focus them, and as

6

it were spray them upon the children, so that they may produce the best possible effect. They are also employed by the teachers in individual cases; if, for example, one scholar in a class does not understand the point put before him, a nature-spirit is at once sent to touch and stimulate a particular centre in his brain, and then in a moment he is able to comprehend. All teachers must be clairvoyant; it is an absolute prerequisite for the office. These teachers are members of the community—men and women indiscriminately; Devas frequently materialize for special occasions or to give certain lessons, but never seem to take the entire responsibility of a school.

The four great types which are symbolized by the Temples are seen to exist here also. The children are carefully observed and treated according to the results of observation. In most cases they sort themselves out at a quite early period into one or other of these lines of development, and every opportunity is given to them to select that which they prefer. Here again there is nothing of the nature of compulsion. Even tiny children are perfectly

acquainted with the object of the community,
and fully realize that it is their duty and their
privilege to order their lives accordingly. It
must be remembered that all these people are
immediate reincarnations, and that most of
them bring over at least some memory of all
their past lives, so that for them education is
simply a process of as rapidly as possible
bringing a new set of vehicles under control
and recovering as quickly as may be any links
that may have been lost in the process of
transition from one physical body to another.

It does not of course in any way follow that
the children of a man who is on (let us say)
the musical line need themselves be musical.
As their previous births are always known to
the parents and schoolmasters, every facility is
given to them to develop either along the line
of their last life or along any other which may
seem to come most easily to them. There is
the fullest co-operation between the parents
and schoolmasters. A particular member who
was noticed took his children to the schoolmaster, explained them all to him in detail,
and constantly visited him to discuss what
might be best for them. If, for example, the

schoolmaster thinks that a certain colour is especially desirable for a particular pupil he communicates his idea to the parents, and much of that colour is put before the child at home as well as at school; he is surrounded with it, and it is used in his dress and so on. All schools are under the direction of the Master K.H., and every schoolmaster is personally responsible to Him.

TRAINING THE IMAGINATION

Let me take as an example the practice of a school attached to one of the yellow Temples, and see how they begin the intellectual development of the lowest class. First the master sets before them a little shining ball, and they are asked to make an image of it in their minds. Some who are quite babies can do it really well. The teacher says:

" You can see my face; now shut your eyes; can you see it still? Now look at this ball; can you shut your eyes and still see it ? "

The teacher, by the use of his clairvoyant faculty, can see whether or not the children

are making satisfactory images. Those who
can do it are set to practise day by day, with
all sorts of simple forms and colours. Then
they are asked to suppose that point moving,
and leaving a track behind it as a shooting star
does ; then to imagine the luminous track, that
is to say, a line. Then they are asked to
imagine this line as moving at right angles to
itself, every point in it leaving a similar track,
and thus they mentally construct for themselves a square. Then all sorts of permutations
and divisions of that square are put before
them. It is broken up into triangles of various
sorts, and it is explained to them that in reality
all these things are living symbols with a
meaning. Even quite the babies are taught
some of these things.

" What does the point mean to you ? "

" One."

" Who is one ? "

" God."

" Where is He ? "

" He is everywhere."

And then presently they learn that two
signifies the duality of Spirit and matter, that
three dots of a certain kind and colour mean

three aspects of the Deity, while three others of a different kind mean the soul in man. A later class has also an intermediate three which obviously mean the Monad. In this way, by associating grand ideas with simple objects, even tiny little children possess an amount of Theosophical information which would seem quite surprising to a person accustomed to an older and less intelligent educational system. An ingenious kind of kindergarten machine was observed, a sort of ivory ball—at least it looked like ivory—which, when a spring is touched, opens out into a cross with a rose drawn upon it like the Rosicrucian symbol, out of which come a number of small balls each of which in turn subdivides. By another movement it can be made to close again, the mechanism being cleverly concealed. This is meant as a symbol to illustrate the idea of the One becoming many, and of the eventual return of the many into the One.

More Advanced Classes

For a later class that luminous square moves again at right angles to itself and produces a cube, and then still later the cube moves at right angles to itself and produces a tesseract, and most of the children are able to see it and to make its image clearly in their minds. Children who have a genius for it are taught to paint pictures, trees and animals, landscapes and scenes from history, and each child is taught to make his picture living. He is taught that the concentration of his thought can actually alter the physical picture, and the children are proud when they can succeed in doing this. Having painted a picture as well as they can, the children concentrate upon it and try to improve it, to modify it by their thought. In a week or so, working at the concentration for some time each day, they are able to produce considerable modifications, and a boy of fourteen can, from much practice, do it quite rapidly.

Having modified his picture, the child is taught to make a thought-form of it, to look at it, to contemplate it earnestly, and then to shut his eyes and visualize it. He takes, first, ordinary physical pictures ; then a glass vessel containing a coloured gas is given to him, and by the effort of his will he has to mould the gas into certain shapes—to make it take a form by thought—to make it become, inside its vessel, a sphere, a cube, a tetrahedron or some such shape. Many children can do this easily after a little practice.

Then they are asked to make it take the shape of a man, and then that of the picture at which they have previously been looking. When they can manage this gaseous matter fairly easily they try to do it in etheric, then in astral, and then in purely mental matter. The teacher himself makes materializations for them to examine when necessary, and in this way they gradually work upward to more advanced acts of thought-creation. All these classes are open to visits from parents and friends, and often many older people like to attend them and themselves practise the exercises set for the children.

THE SCHOOL SYSTEM

There is nothing in the nature of the boarding-school, and all children live happily at home and attend the school which is most convenient for them. In a few cases the

Deva-priests are training children to take their places ; but even in these cases the child is not taken away from home, though he is usually surrounded by a special protective shell, so that other vibrations may not interfere with the influence which the Deva pours in upon him.

A child does not belong to a class at all in the same way as under older methods ; each child has a list of numbers for different subjects ; he may be in the first class for one subject, in the third for another, in the fifth for some other. Even for small children the arrangement seems to be far less a class than a kind of lecture-room. In trying to comprehend the system, we must never for a moment forget the effect of the immediate reincarnations, and that consequently not only are these children on the average far more intelligent and developed than other children of their age, but also they are unequally developed. Some children of four remember more of a previous incarnation, and of what they learnt then, than other children of eight or nine ; and again some children remember a certain subject fully and clearly, and yet have almost entirely lost their knowledge of some other subjects which seem quite as easy. So that we are dealing with entirely abnormal conditions, and the schemes adopted have to be suited to them.

At what corresponds to the opening of the school, they all stand together and sing something. They have four lessons in their morning session, but the lessons are short, and there is always an interval for play between them. Like all their houses, the school-room has no walls, but is supported entirely on pillars, so that practically the whole life of the children, as well as of the rest of the community, is lived in the open air; but nevertheless the children are turned out even from that apology for a room after each of the lessons, and left to play about in the park which surrounds the school. Girls and boys are taught together promiscuously. This morning session covers all of what would be called the compulsory subjects—the subjects which everybody learns; there are some extra lessons in the afternoon on additional subjects for those who wish to take them, but a considerable number of the children are satisfied with the morning work.

The Curriculum

The school curriculum is different from that of the twentieth century. The very subjects are mostly different, and even those which are the same are taught in an entirely different way. Arithmetic, for example, has been greatly simplified; there are no complex weights and measures of any kind, everything being arranged on a decimal system; they calculate but little, and the detailed working-out of long rows of figures would be denounced as insufferably tedious. Nothing is taught but what is likely to be practically useful to the average person in after-life; all the rest is a matter of reference.

In earlier centuries they had books of logarithms, by reference to which long and complicated calculations could be avoided; now they have the same system immensely extended, and yet, at the same time, much more compressed. It is a scheme by which the result of practically any difficult calculation can be looked up in a few moments by a person who knows the book. The children know how to calculate, just as a man may know how to make his own logarithms, and yet habitually use a book for them to avoid the waste of time in tedious processes involving long rows of figures.

Arithmetic with them is hardly a subject in itself, but is taken only as leading up to calculations connected with the geometry which deals with solid figures and the higher dimensions. The whole thing is so different from previous ideas that it is not easy to describe it clearly. For example, in all the children's sums there is no question of money, and no complicated calculation. To understand the sum and know how to do it is sufficient. The theory in the schoolmaster's mind is not to cram the brains of the children, but to develop their faculties and tell them where to find facts. Nobody, for example, would think of multiplying a line of six figures by another similar line, but would employ either a calculating machine (for these are common), or one of the books to which I have referred.

The whole problem of reading and writing is far simpler than it used to be, for all spelling is phonetic, and pronunciation cannot be wrong when a certain syllable must always

have a certain sound. The writing has somewhat the appearance of shorthand. There is
a good deal to learn in it, but at the same time,
when he has learnt it, the child is in possession of a finer and more flexible instrument
than any of the older languages, since he can
write at least as fast as any ordinary person
can speak. There is a large amount of convention about it, and a whole sentence is often
expressed by a mark like a flash of lightning.

The language which they are speaking is
naturally English, since the community has
arisen in an English-speaking country, but it
has been modified considerably. Many parti-
cipial forms have disappeared, and some of the
words are different. All subjects are learnt
so differently now. Nobody learns any
history, except isolated interesting stories, but
everyone has in his house a book in which an
epitome of all history can be found. Geography is still learnt to a limited extent.
They know where all the different races live,
and with great precision in what these races
differ, and what qualities they are developing.
But the commercial side has dropped; no one
bothers about the exports of Bulgaria; nobody

knows where they make woollen cloth, or wants to know. All these things can be turned up at a moment's notice in books which are part of the free furniture of every house, and it would be considered a waste of time to burden the memory with such valueless facts.

The scheme is in every respect strictly utilitarian; they do not teach the children anything which can be easily obtained from an encyclopædia. They have developed a scheme of restricting education to necessary and valuable knowledge. A boy of twelve usually has behind him, in his physical brain, the entire memory of what he knew in previous lives. It is the custom to carry a talisman over from life to life, which helps the child to recover the memory in the new vehicles—a talisman which he wore in his previous birth, so that it is thoroughly loaded with the magnetism of that birth and can now stir up again the same vibrations.

CHILDREN'S SERVICES

Another interesting educational feature is what is called the children's service at the

Temple. Many others than children attend this, especially those who are not yet quite up to the level of the other services already described. The children's service in the music-Temple is exceedingly beautiful; the children perform a series of graceful evolutions, and both sing and play upon instruments as they march about. That in the colour-Temple is something like an especially gorgeous Drury Lane pantomime, and has evidently been many times carefully rehearsed.

In one case they are reproducing the choric dance of the priests of Babylon, which represents the movement of the planets round the sun. This is performed upon an open plain, as it used to be in Assyria, and groups of children dress in special colours (representing the various planets) and move harmoniously, so that in their play they have also an astronomical lesson. But it must be understood that they fully feel that they are engaging in a sacred religious rite, and that to do it well and thoroughly will not only be helpful to themselves, but that it also constitutes a kind of offering of their services to the Deity. They have been told that this used to be done in an old religion many thousands of years ago.

The children take great delight in it, and there is quite a competition to be chosen to be part of the Sun! Proud parents also look on, and are pleased to be able to say : " My boy is part of Mercury to-day," and so on. The planets all have their satellites—more satellites in some cases than used to be known, so that astronomy has evidently progressed. The rings of Saturn are remarkably well represented by a number of children in constant motion in a figure closely resembling the ' grand chain ' at the commencement of the fifth figure of the Lancers. An especially interesting point is that even the inner ' crape ' ring of Saturn is represented, for those children who are on the inside of the next ring keep a gauzy garment floating out so as to represent it. The satellites are single children or pairs of children waltzing outside the ring. All the while, though they enjoy it immensely, they never forget that they are performing a religious function and that they are offering this to God. Another dance evidently indicates the transfer of life from the Moon Chain to the Earth Chain. All sorts of instruction is given to the children in this way, half a play and half a religious ceremony.

SYMBOLIC DANCES

There are great festivals which each Temple celebrates by special performances of this kind, and on these occasions they all do their best in the way of gorgeous decoration. The buildings are so arranged that the lines are picked out in a kind of permanent phosphorescence, not a line of lamps, but a glow which seems to come from the substance. The lines of the architecture are graceful, and this has a splendid effect. The children's service is an education in colours. The combinations are really wonderful, and the drilling of the children is perfect. Great masses of them are dressed identically in the most lovely hues, delicate and yet brilliant, and they move in and out among one another in the most complicated figures.

In their choric dance they are taught that they must not only wear the colour of the star for spectacular purposes, but

7

must also try mentally to make the same colour. They are instructed to try to fancy themselves that colour, and try to think that they actually are part of the planet Mercury or Venus, as the case may be. As they move they sing and play, each planet having its own special chords, so that all the planets as they go round the sun may produce an imitation of the music of the spheres. In these children's services also the Devas often take part, and aid with the colours and the music. Both kāma and rūpa Devas move quite freely among the people, and take part in daily life.

The children's service in connection with the yellow Temple is exceedingly interesting. Here they dance frequently in geometrical figures, but the evolutions are difficult to describe. One performance, for example, is exceedingly pretty and effective. Thirty-two boys wearing golden brocaded robes are arranged in a certain order, not all standing on the same level, but on raised stages. They evidently represent the angles of some solid figure. They hold in their hands thick ropes of a golden-coloured thread, and they hold these ropes from one to another so as to indicate the outline of a certain figure—say a dodecahedron.

Suddenly, at a preconcerted signal, they drop one end of the rope or throw it to another boy, and in a moment the outline has changed into that of an icosahedron. This is wonderfully effective, and gives quite a remarkable illusory effect of changing solid figures one into another. All such changes are gone through in a certain order, which is somehow connected with the evolution of the matter of the planes at the commencement of a solar system. Another movement is evidently to illustrate something of the formation of atoms out of bubbles. The children represent bubbles. A number of them rush out from the centre and arrange themselves in a certain way. Then they rush back again to the centre and again come still further out, and group themselves in quite a different way. All this needs much training, but the children appear most enthusiastic about it.

THE UNDERLYING IDEA

The education and the religion are so closely mingled that it is difficult clearly to differentiate

one from the other. The children are playing in the Temple. The underlying idea
which is kept before them is that all this is
only the physical side of something far greater
and grander, which belongs to higher worlds,
so that they feel that to everything they do
there is an inner side, and they hope to
realize this and to be able to see and comprehend it directly; and this is always held
before them as the final reward of their
efforts.

BIRTH AND DEATH

The various influences which take such a
prominent part in the education of the children
are brought to bear upon them even before
birth. Once more we must reiterate that
when a birth is about to take place the father
and mother and all parties concerned are quite
aware what ego is to come to them, and
therefore they take care that for months
before the actual birth takes place the surroundings shall in every way be suitable to that
ego, and such as may conduce to a perfect
physical body.

Great stress is laid upon the influence of beautiful surroundings. The future mother has always before her eyes lovely pictures and graceful statues. The whole of life is pervaded with this idea of beauty —so much so that it would be considered a crime against the community that any object should be ugly or ungraceful. In all architecture this beauty of line as well as of colour is the first consideration, and the same is true with regard to all the minor accessories of life. Even before the child's birth preparation will be made for him; his mother dresses chiefly in certain colours, and surrounds herself with flowers and lights of what are considered the most appropriate kind.

Parentage is a matter of arrangement between all parties concerned, and death is usually voluntary. As the members of this community live entirely healthy lives, and have surrounded themselves with perfect sanitary conditions, disease has been practically eliminated, so that except in the rare case of an accident no one dies except of old age, and they do not drop the body as long as it is useful. They do not feel at all that they are giving up life, but only that they are changing a worn-out vehicle. The absence of worry and unhealthy conditions has certainly tended on the whole to lengthen physical life. Nobody looks at all old until at least eighty, and many pass beyond the century.

When a man begins to find his powers failing him, he also begins to look round him for a desirable re-birth. He selects a father and mother whom he thinks would suit him, and goes round to call upon them to ask whether they are willing to take him. If they are, he tells them that he expects to die soon, and then hands over to them his personal talisman which he has worn all his life, and also sends to them any personal effects which he wishes to carry over to his next life. The talisman is usually a jewel of the particular type appropriate to the ego, according to the sign of the Zodiac to which as an ego he belongs, the influence under which he attained individuality. This charm he always wears, so that it may be fully impregnated with his magnetism, and he is careful to make arrangements that it may be handed over to him in his next birth, in order to help in the arousing in the new body of the memory of past lives, so as to make it easier to keep unbroken the realization of life as an ego.

This amulet is always correspondent to his name as an ego—the name which he carries with him from life to life. In many cases men are already using this name in ordinary life, though in others they have perpetuated the name which they bore when they entered the community, carrying it on from life to life and altering its termination so as to make it masculine or feminine according to the sex of the moment. Each person has therefore his own name, his permanent name, and in addition in each incarnation he takes that of the family into which he happens or chooses to be born.

The personal effects do not include anything of the nature of money, for money is no longer used, and no man has more than a life-interest in houses or land, or in other property. But he has sometimes a few books or ornaments which he wishes to preserve, and if so he hands them over to his prospective father and mother, who, when they hear that his death is approaching, can begin to prepare for him. He does not alter his ordinary mode of life; he does nothing which in the slightest degree resembles committing suicide; but he simply loses the will to live—lets his life go, as it were—and generally passes away peacefully in sleep within a short period of time. Usually, indeed, he takes up his abode with the prospective father and mother as soon as the agreement is made, and dies at their house.

There is no funeral ceremony of any sort, as death is not regarded as an event of any importance. The body is not cremated, but is instead placed in a kind of retort into which some chemical is poured—probably a strong acid of some sort. The retort is then hermetically sealed, and a power resembling electricity, but far stronger, is passed through it. The acid fizzes vigorously, and in a few minutes the whole body is entirely dissolved. When the retort is opened and the process is completed there is nothing left but a fine grey powder. This is not preserved or regarded with any reverence. The operation of disposing of the body is easily performed at the house, the apparatus being brought there when desired. There is no ceremony of any kind, and the friends of the deceased do not assemble for the occasion.

They do, however, come round and pay him a visit soon after his rebirth, as the sight of them is supposed to help to re-awaken the memory in the new baby body. Under these circumstances there are of course no prayers or ceremonies of any kind for the dead, nor is there any need of help upon the astral plane, for every member of the community remembers his past lives and knows perfectly well the body which he is about to take as soon as it can be prepared for him. Many members of the community continue to act as invisible helpers to the rest of the world, but within the community itself nothing of that kind is necessary.

The Manu has a careful record kept of all the successive incarnations of each of the members of His community, and in some rare cases He interferes with an ego's choice of his parents. As a general rule all the members of the community have already disposed of such grosser karma as would limit them in their choice, and they also know enough of their own type and of the conditions which they require not to make an unsuitable selection, so that in almost every case they are left perfectly free to make their own arrangements. The matter is, however, always within the knowledge of the Manu, so that He may alter the plan if He does not approve.

As a rule the dying man is at liberty to select the sex of his next birth, and many people seem to make a practice of taking birth alternately as man and as woman. There is no actual regulation as to this, and everything is left as free as possible; but at the same time the due proportion of the sexes in the community must be maintained, and if the number of either sex falls temporarily below what it should be, the Manu calls for volunteers to bring things once more into harmony. Parents usually arrange to have ten or twelve children in the family, and generally the same number of girls as boys. Twins, and even triplets, are not at all uncommon. Between the birth of one child and the next there is mostly an interval of two or three years, and there are evidently theories with regard to this matter.

The great object is to produce perfect children, and no cripples or deformed persons are to be seen, nor is there any infant mortality. It is manifest that the labour of child-birth has diminished almost to vanishing-point; indeed, there seems to be scarcely any trouble, except perhaps a little with the first child.

MARRIAGE

This brings us to the question of marriage. There is no restriction placed upon this, except the one great restriction that no one must marry outside the community; but it is generally regarded as rather undesirable that people of the same type of religious feeling should intermarry. There is no rule against it, but it is understood that on the whole the Manu prefers that it should not take place, though He does not refuse His sanction to it in cases where there is an irresistible attraction. But there is a certain all-sufficing expression which practically puts any matter beyond the limits of discussion: " It is not His wish."

People choose their own partners for life— fall in love, in fact—much as they used to do, but the dominant idea of duty is always supreme, and even in matters of the heart no one permits himself to do anything or feel anything which he does not think to be for the best for the community. The great motive is not passion, but duty. The ordinary sex passions have been dominated, so that people now unite themselves definitely with a view to carrying on the community and to creating good bodies for the purpose. They regard married life chiefly as an opportunity to that end, and what is necessary for such production is a religious and magical action which needs to be carefully directed. It forms part of the sacrifice of themselves to the LOGOS, so that no one must lose his balance or his reason in connection with it.

When people fall in love, and, as we should say, engage themselves, they go to the Manu Himself and ask Him for a benediction on their union. Usually they also arrange with a prospective son or daughter, so that when they go to the Manu they say that such and such a man wishes to be born from them, and ask that they may be permitted to marry. The Manu examines them to see whether

they will suit each other, and if He approves
He pronounces for them a formula : " Your
life together shall be blessed." Marriage is
regarded almost entirely from the point of
view of the prospective offspring. Sometimes
it is even arranged by them. One man will
call on another and say :

" I am expecting to die in a few weeks, and
I should like to have you and Miss X. for my
father and mother, as I have some kārmic ties
with both of you that I should like to work
off ; would that be agreeable to you ? "

Not infrequently the suggestion seems to be
accepted, and the plan works out well. One
man, who was taken at random for the purpose of investigation, was found to have three
egos desiring to incarnate through him, so
that when he took his prospective wife to the
Manu he asked :

" May we two marry, with these three egos
waiting to take birth through us ? "

And the Manu gave His consent. There is
no other marriage ceremony than this benediction given by the Manu, nor is a wedding
made the occasion of feasting or the giving
of presents. There is nothing in the nature

of a marriage contract. The arrangements are exclusively monogamous, and there is no such thing as divorce, though the agreement is always terminable by mutual consent. People marry distinctly with a view of furnishing a vehicle for a certain soul, and when that is safely done it seems to be entirely at their option whether they renew their agreement or not. Since the parents are selected with care, in the majority of cases the agreement is renewed, and they remain as husband and wife for life ; but there are cases in which the agreement is terminated, and both parties form other alliances. Here also, as in everything else, duty is the one ruling factor, and everyone is always ready to yield his personal preference to what is thought to be best for the community as a whole. There is therefore far less of passion in these lives than in those of the older centuries; and the strongest affection is probably that between parents and children.

There are cases in which the unwritten rule as to not marrying a person of the same type is abrogated, as, for example, when it is desired to produce children who can be trained by the Devas as priests for a particular Temple. In the rare case where a man is killed by some accident, he is at once impounded in the astral body and arrangements are made for his re-birth. Large numbers of people desire to be born as children of the members of the Council; those, however, have only the usual number of children, lest the quality should be deteriorated. Birth in the family of the Manu Himself is the greatest of all honours; but of course He selects His children Himself.

There is no difference of status between the sexes, and they take up indifferently any work that is to be done. On this matter it may be interesting to record the opinion of a mind of that period which was examined for that special purpose. This man does not seem to think much of the difference between man and woman. He says that there must be both, in order that the Race may be founded, but that we know there is a better time coming for the women. He feels that in bearing children the women are taking a harder share of the work, and are therefore to be pitied and protected. The Council, however, is composed entirely of men, and, under the direction of the Manu, its members are making experiments in the creation of mind-born bodies. They have produced some respectable copies of humanity, but have not yet succeeded in satisfying the Manu.

CHAPTER V

BUILDINGS AND CUSTOMS

RACIAL CHARACTERISTICS

IN appearance the community is still like the sixth sub-race from which it sprang—that is to say, it is a white Race, although there are among it people with darker hair and eyes and a Spanish or Italian complexion. The stature of the Race has distinctly increased, for none of the men are under six feet, and even the women are but little short of this. The people are all muscular and well-proportioned, and much attention is paid to exercise and the equal development of the muscles. It is noteworthy that they preserve a free and graceful carriage even to extreme old age.

8

PUBLIC BUILDINGS

It was mentioned in the beginning that when the community was founded a vast block of central buildings was erected, and that the houses of the first settlers were grouped round that, though always with ample space batween them for beautiful gardens. By this time many subordinate towns have sprung up in the district—though perhaps the word town may mislead a twentieth-century reader, since there is nothing in the least resembling the sort of town to which he is accustomed. The settlements may rather be called groups of villas thinly scattered amidst lovely parks and gardens ; but at least all such settlements have their Temples, so that every inhabitant is always within easy reach of a Temple of the variety which he happens to prefer. The inhabited part of the estate is not of great size, some forty or fifty miles in diameter, so that even the great central buildings are, after all, quite easily available for anyone who wishes to visit them. Each Temple has usually in its neighbourhood a block of other public buildings

—a sort of public hall, an extensive library, and also a set of school-buildings.

HOUSES

The houses built for the community before its foundation were all on the same general plan and, though a good deal of individual taste has been shown in those erected since, the broad principle is still the same. The two great features of their architecture which much differentiate it from almost all that preceded it, are the absence of walls and of corners. Houses, temples, schools, factories, all of them are nothing but roofs supported upon pillars—pillars in most cases as lofty as those of the Egyptian Temples, though far lighter and more graceful. There is, however, provision for closing the spaces between the pillars when necessary—something distantly resembling the patent automatic rolling shop-blinds of earlier centuries, but they can be made transparent at will. These devices, however, are rarely employed, and the whole of the life of the people, night and day, is in reality spent in the open air.

Domes of many shapes and sizes are prominent features. Some of them are of the shape of that of St. Peter's, though smaller; some are low and broad, like those of San Giovanni degli Eremiti, in Palermo; some with the lotus-bud shape of those of a Muhammadan mosque. These domes are full of windows, or are often themselves built of some transparent substance of various colours. Every Temple has a great central dome, and every house has one at least. The general scheme of the house is to have a sort of great circular or oval hall under the dome, which is the general living room. Fully three-fourths of its circumference is quite open, but behind the fourth part are often built rooms and offices of various kinds, which usually rise to only half the height of the columns, having above them other small rooms which are used as bedrooms by those who desire privacy.

All those rooms, though separated from one another by partitions, have no outside walls, so that in them also people are still practically in the open air. There are no corners anywhere, every room being circular

or oval. There is always some part of the
roof upon which it is possible to walk. Every
house is full of flowers and statues, and another
striking feature is the abundance of water
everywhere; there are fountains, artificial
cascades, miniature lakes and pools in all
directions.

The houses are always lighted from the
roof. No lamps or lanterns are seen, but the
dome is made to glow out in a mass of light,
the colour of which can be changed at will,
and in the smaller rooms a section of the
ceiling is arranged to glow in the same way.
All the parks and streets are thoroughly
lighted at night with a soft and moonlike but
penetrating light—a far nearer approach to
daylight than anything previously secured.

FURNISHING

Furniture is principally conspicuous by its
absence. There are scarcely any chairs in
the houses, and there are no seats of any sort
in the Temples or public halls. The people
recline upon cushions somewhat in the
oriental style, or rather perhaps like the ancient

Romans, for they do not usually sit cross-legged. The cushions, however, are curious; they are always either air-cushions or entirely vegetable products stuffed with some especially soft fibrous material, not altogether unlike coconut fibre. These things are washable, and indeed are constantly being washed. When going to the Temple, to the library or to any public meeting each person usually carries his own air-cushion with him, but in the houses large numbers are seen lying about which may be used by anybody.

There are small low tables—or perhaps they are rather to be described as book-rests, which can be so arranged as to be flat like a table. All the floors are of marble, or of stone polished like marble—often a rich crimson hue. Beds, filled either with air or water, or made of the same vegetable material as that used for the cushions, are laid upon the floor, or sometimes suspended like hammocks, but no bedsteads are used. In the few cases where there are comparatively permanent walls, as for example between the bedrooms and offices and the great hall, they are always beautifully painted with landscapes and historic scenes. Curiously, all these things are interchangeable, and there is a department which is always prepared to arrange exchanges—a kind of circulating library for decorations, through the medium of which any person can change the wall-panels or statues which decorate his house, whenever he wishes to do so.

DRESS

The dress of the people is simple and graceful, but at the same time strictly utilitarian. Most of it is not unlike that of India, though we sometimes see an approach to the ancient Greek dress. There is no uniformity about it, and people wear all sorts of different things. But there is nothing inharmonious; all is in perfect taste. Colours both brilliant and delicate are worn by both men and women alike, for there seems to be no distinction between the clothing of the sexes. Not a single article is made of wool; it is never worn.

The substance employed is exclusively linen or cotton, but it is steeped in some chemical which preserves its fibres so that the garments

last for a long time, even though all are washed daily. The ·chemical process imparts a
glossy satin-like surface, but does not interfere
in the least with the softness or flexibility of
the material. No shoes or sandals or any
other foot-coverings are worn by the members
of the community, and scarcely any people
wear hats, though there are a few something
like the panama, and one or two small linen
caps were seen. The idea of distinctive
clothes for certain offices has disappeared ; no
uniforms of any sort are worn, except that the
officiating Deva always materializes round
himself robes of the colour of his Temple,
while conducting a service ; and the children,
as before described, dress themselves in certain
colours when they are about to take part in
the religious festivals.

FOOD

The community is entirely vegetarian,
because it is one of the standing rules that
nothing must be killed. Even the outer world
is by this time largely vegetarian, because
people have begun to recognize that the eating

of flesh is coarse, vulgar, and above all un-
fashionable! Comparatively few take the
trouble of preparing their own meals, or eat
in their own houses, though they are perfectly
free to do so if they wish. Most go to what
may be called restaurants, although, as they
are practically entirely in the open air, they
may be supposed rather to resemble tea-
gardens. Fruit enters largely into the diet of
the period. We have a bewildering variety
of fruits, and centuries of care have been
devoted to scientific crossing of fruits, so as to
produce the most perfect forms of nourish-
ment and to give them at the same time
remarkable flavours.

If we look in at a fruit-farm we see that the
section devoted to each kind of fruit is always
divided into smaller sections, and each section
is labelled as having a particular flavour. We
may have, for example, grapes or apples, let
us say, with a strawberry flavour, a clove
flavour, a vanilla flavour, and so on—mixtures
which would seem curious from the point of
view of those who are not accustomed to them.
This is a country where there is almost no
rain, so that all cultivation is managed by

means of irrigation, and as they irrigate these different sections they throw into the water what is called 'plant-food' and by variations in this they succeed in imparting different flavours. By varying the food, growth can be intensified or retarded, and the size of the fruits can also be regulated. The estate of the community runs up into the hills, so they have the opportunity at different levels of cultivating almost all possible kinds of fruit.

The food which is most eaten is a sort of substance somewhat resembling blanc-mange. It is to be had in all kinds of colourings, and the colouring indicates the flavour, just as it used to do in ancient Peru. There is a large selection. Perhaps the choice of different flavours in the food may to some extent take the place of many habits which have now disappeared, such as smoking, wine-drinking, or the eating of sweets. There is also a substance which looks like cheese, but is sweet. It is certainly not cheese, for no animal products are used, and no animals are kept in the colony except as pets. Milk is used, but it is exclusively the vegetable milk obtained from what is sometimes called the cow-tree, or an exact imitation made from some kind of bean.

Knives and forks do not appear, but spoons are still used, and most people bring their own with them. The attendant has a sort of weapon like a hatchet with which he opens fruits and nuts. It is made of an alloy which has all the qualities of gold but has a hard edge, which apparently does not need resharpening. It is possibly made of one of the rarer metals, such as iridium. In these restaurant gardens also there are no chairs, but each person half-reclines in a marble depression in the ground, and there is a marble slab which can be turned round in front of him so that he can put his food upon it, and when he has finished he turns this up and water flows over it.

On the whole people eat distinctly less than in the twentieth century. The usual custom is to have one regular meal in the middle of the day, and to take a light refection of fruit in the morning and evening. Everybody is at breakfast just after sunrise, for people are always up then or a little before. The light evening meal is at about five o'clock,

for most people go to bed fairly early. So far
as has been seen, no one sits down to a heavy
meal in the evening; but there is complete
individual freedom with regard to all these
matters, so that people follow their own taste.
The drinking of tea or coffee has not been
observed; indeed there seems to be but little
drinking of any sort, possibly because so much
fruit is eaten.

Plenty of water is available everywhere,
even though there is almost no rain. They
have enormous works for the distillation of
sea-water, which is raised to a great height
and then sent out on a most liberal scale. It
is worthy of note, however, that the water
specially sent out for drinking is not the pure
result of the distillation, but they add to it a
small proportion of certain chemicals—the
theory being that pure distilled water is not
the most healthy for drinking purposes. The
manager of the distillation-works explains
that they use natural spring water as far as it
will go, but they cannot find nearly enough
of it, and so it has to be supplemented by the
distilled water; but then it is necessary
to add the chemicals to this in order to

make it fresh and sparkling and really thirst-quenching.

LIBRARIES

The literary arrangements are curious but perfect. Every house is provided, gratis and as part of its permanent fittings, with a sort of encyclopædia of the most comprehensive nature, containing an epitome of practically all that is known, put as tersely as possible and yet with great wealth of detail, so as to contain all the information that an ordinary man is ever likely to want on any subject. If, however, for some reason he needs to know more, he has only to go to the nearest district-library, of which there is one connected with each Temple. There he finds a far fuller encyclopædia, in which the article on any given subject contains a careful epitome of every book that has ever been written upon it—a most colossal work. If he wants to know still more, or if he wants to consult original books printed in the old languages or the ancient Roman type now disused, he has to go to the central library of the community, which is on a scale commensurate with that of the British Museum. Translations into the English of the day printed in this shorthand-like script are always appended to these originals.

Thus it is possible for a man to study to the fullest any subject in which he is interested, for all instruments of research and books are provided free in this way. New books are being written all the time on all conceivable subjects. The fiction of the day is almost entirely based upon reincarnation, the characters always passing from life to life and exemplifying the working of karma; but a novelist in these days writes not with a view to fame or money, but always to the good of the community. Some people are writing short articles, and these are always on view at their own district Temple hall. Anyone may go and read them there, and anyone who is interested has only to go and ask for a copy and it is given to him. If a man is writing a book it is exhibited in this way, chapter by chapter; the whole life is in this way communal; the people share with their neighbours what they are doing while they are doing it.

Newspapers

The daily newspaper has disappeared—or perhaps we may rather say that it survives in a much amended form. To make it comprehensible it must be premised that in each house there is a machine which is a kind of combination of a telephone and recording tape-machine. This is in connection with a central office in the capital city, and is so arranged that not only can one speak through it as though a telephone, but that anything written or drawn upon a specially prepared plate and put into the box of the large machine at the central office will reproduce itself automatically upon slips which fall into the box of the machine in each of the houses.

What takes the place of the morning newspaper is managed in this way. It may be said that each person has his newspaper printed in his own house. When any news of importance arrives at any time it is instantly forwarded in this way to every house in the community; but a special collection of such news is sent early each morning and is commonly called the *Community Breakfast*

Chat. It is a comparatively small affair and has a certain resemblance to a table of contents and an index, for it gives the briefest epitome of the news, but attaches a number to each item, the different departments being printed upon different colours. If any person wants full information as to any of the items, he has only to ring up the central office and ask for details of number so-and-so, and all that is available is at once sent along his wire and dropped before him.

But the newspaper differs greatly from those of older times. There is hardly any political news, for even the outer world has changed in many ways. There is a great deal of information upon scientific subjects, and as to new theories. There are still notes of the private doings of royal people, but they are quite brief. There is a department for community news, but even that is chiefly concerned with scientific papers, inventions and discoveries, although it also records marriages and births.

The same instrument is also used for adding to the household encyclopædias whenever it is necessary. Extra slips are sent out daily whenever there is anything to say, so that just as the newspaper is being delivered in slices all day, so now and then come little slips to be added to the various departments of the encyclopædia.

PUBLIC MEETINGS

In connection with each Temple there is a definite scheme of educational buildings, so that broadly speaking the school-work of each district is done under the ægis of its Temple. The great central Temple has in connection with it the huge open-air places of assembly, where, when necessary, almost the entire community can be gathered together. More usually, when the Manu desires to promulgate some edict or information to all His people He Himself speaks in the great central Temple, and what He says is simultaneously produced by a sort of altogether improved phonographic system in all the other Temples. It would seem that each of the district Temples has a sort of representative phonograph in the central Temple, which records at the other end of the line all that takes place there, so that all particulars are in this way immediately reproduced.

9

SCIENCE DEPARTMENTS

Mention has already been made of the great central library in connection with the central Temple. In addition to that, as another part of the same great mass of buildings, there is a complete and well-appointed museum, and also what may be called a university. Many branches of study are taken up here, but they are pursued by methods different from those of old. The study of animals and plants, for example, is entirely and only done by means of clairvoyance, and never by destruction of any kind, only those being professors and students of these arts who have developed sufficient sight to work in this manner. There is a department of what we may call physical geography, which has already mapped out the entire earth in a vast number of large-scale models, which show by coloured signs and inscriptions not only the nature of the surface soil, but also what is to be found in the way of minerals and fossils down to a considerable depth.

There is also an elaborate ethnographical department in which there are life-size statues

of all races of men which have ever existed
on the earth, and also models of those existing
on other planets of this chain. There is even
a department with reference to the other
chains of the solar system. For each of the
statues there is an exhaustive description with
diagrams showing in what way his higher
vehicles differ. The whole is tabulated and
arranged from the point of view of the Manu,
to show what the development of mankind has
been in the various Races and sub-races. A
good deal is also shown of the future, and
models with detailed explanations are given
for them also.

In addition to this there is also the ana-
tomical department, dealing with the whole
detailed anatomy of the human and animal
bodies in the past, the present and the
future. There is not exactly any medical
department, for illness no longer exists; it
has been eliminated. There is still, however,
surgery for cases of accident, though even that
has been much improved. Few professors of
that art are needed, for naturally accidents are
rare. There is nothing corresponding to the
great hospitals of former times, but only a few

light and airy rooms, in which the victims of accidents can be temporarily laid if necessary.

Connected with the centre of learning is also an elaborate museum of all sorts of arts and crafts which have existed in the world from the beginning onwards. There are also models of all kinds of machinery, most of which is new to us, since it has been invented between the twentieth century and the twenty-eighth. There is also much Atlantean machinery which had long been forgotten, so that there is a complete arrangement for any kind of study along these lines.

History is still being written, and it has been in process of production for more than a hundred years; but it is being written from a reading of the records. It is illustrated by a method which is quite new to us—a method which precipitates a scene from the records when it is considered important. We have in addition a series of models illustrating the history of the world at all periods. In the central library there are certain small rooms somewhat like telephone-cabinets, into which students can take the record of any prominent event in history, and by putting it into a

machine and setting that in motion they can
have the whole scene reproduced audibly and
visibly, with the exact presentment of the
appearance of the actors, and their words in
the very tones in which they were spoken.

There is also an astronomical department,
with most interesting machinery indicating
the exact position at any moment of everything visible in the sky. There is a great
mass of information about all these worlds.
There are two departments, one for direct
observation by various means and another for
the tabulation of information acquired by
testimony. Much of this information has been
given by Devas connected with various planets
and stars; but this is always kept entirely
apart from the results of direct observation.
Chemistry has been carried to a wonderful
height and depth. All possible combinations
are now fully understood, and the science has
an extension in connection with elemental
essence, which leads on to the whole question
of nature-spirits and Devas as a definite
department of science, studied with illustrative
models. There is also a department of talis-
mans, so that any sensitive person can by

psychometry go behind the mere models, and see the things in themselves.

ARTS

It does not seem that lecturing holds at all a prominent place. Sometimes a man who is studying a subject may talk to a few friends about it, but beyond that, if he has anything to say he submits it to the officials and it is included in the daily news. If anybody writes poetry or an essay he communicates it to his own family, and perhaps puts it up in the district hall. People still paint, but only as a kind of recreation. No one now devotes the whole of his time to that. Art, however, permeates life to a far greater extent than ever before, for everything, even the simplest object for daily use, is artistically made, and the people put something of themselves into their work and are always trying new experiments.

There is nothing corresponding to a theatre, and on bringing the idea to the notice of an inhabitant, a definition of it comes into his mind as a place in which people used to run

about and declaim, pretending to be other than
they were, and taking the parts of great people.
They consider it as archaic and childish. The
great choric dances and processions may be
considered as theatrical, but to them these
appear as religious exercises.

Games and athletics are prominent in this
new life. There are gymnasiums, and much
attention is given to physical development in
women as well as in men. A game much
like lawn-tennis is one of the principal favour-
ites. The children play about just as of old,
and enjoy great freedom.

WILL-POWER

The force of will is universally recognized
in the community and many things are performed by its direct action. Nature-spirits
are well known, and take a prominent part in
the daily life of the people, most of whom can
see them. Almost all children are able to see
them and to use them in various ways, but
they often lose some of this power as they
grow up. The use of such methods, and also
of telepathy, is a kind of game among the

children, and the grown-up people recognize their superiority in this respect, so that if they want to convey a message to some friend at a distance they often call the nearest child and ask him to send it rather than attempt to do it themselves. He can send the message telepathically to some child at the other end, who then immediately conveys it to the person for whom it is intended, and this is a quite reliable and usual method of communication. Adults often lose the power at the time of their marriage, but some few of them retain it, though it needs a far greater effort for them than it does for the child.

ECONOMIC CONDITIONS

Some effort was made to comprehend the economic conditions of the colony, but it was not found easy to understand them. The community is self-supporting, making for itself everything which it needs. The only importations from outside are curiosities such as ancient manuscripts, books and objects of art. These are always paid for by the officials of the community, who have a certain amount of the money of the outside world, which has been brought in by tourists or visitors. Also they have learnt the secret of making gold and jewels of various kinds by alchemical means, and these are often used for payment for the few goods imported from the outside. If a private member wishes for something which can only be bought from the outer world, he gives notice of his desire to the nearest official, and work of some sort is assigned to him in addition to the daily work which he is normally doing, so that by that he may earn the value of whatever he desires.

Everybody undertakes some work for the good of the community, but it is usually left entirely to each to choose what it is to be. No one kind of work is esteemed nobler than any other kind, and there is no idea of caste of any sort. The child at a certain age chooses what he will do, and it is always open to him to change from one kind of work to another by giving due notice. Education is free, but the free tuition of the central university is given only to those who have already shown themselves specially proficient in the branches which they wish to pursue. Food and clothing are given freely to all—or rather, to each person is distributed periodically a number of tokens in exchange for one of which he can obtain a meal at any of the great restaurant-gardens anywhere all over the colony. Or if he prefers it he can go to certain great stores and there obtain food-materials, which he can take home and prepare as he wishes. The arrangement appears complicated to an outsider, but it works perfectly simply among those who thoroughly understand it.

All the people are working for the community, and among the work done is the production of food and clothing, which it then proceeds to hand round. Take, for example, the case of a cloth factory. It is the Government's factory, and it is turning out on an average so much cloth, but the output can be increased or decreased at will. The work is chiefly in the hands of girls, who join the factory voluntarily; indeed, there is a competition to obtain places, for only a certain number are needed. If things are not wanted they are not made. If cloth is wanted the factory is there to produce it; if not, it simply waits. The superintendent in charge of the cloth-store of the Government calculates that in a certain time he will need so much cloth, that he has in stock so much, and therefore requires for renewal so much, and he asks for it accordingly; if he does not want any, he says he has enough. The factory never closes, though the hours vary considerably.

In this cloth factory the workers are mostly women, quite young, and they are doing little but superintending certain machines and seeing that they do not go wrong. Each of them is managing a kind of loom into which she has put a number of patterns. Imagine something like a large clock-face with a number of movable studs on it. When a girl starts her machine she arranges these studs according to her own ideas, and as the machine goes on its movements produce a certain design. She can set it to turn out fifty cloths, each of different pattern, and then leave it. Each girl sets her machine differently—that is where their art comes in; every piece is different from every other piece, unless she allows the machine to run through its list over again after it has finished the fifty. In the meantime, after having started the machines the girls need only to glance at them occasionally, and the machinery is so perfect that practically nothing ever goes wrong with it. It is arranged to run almost silently, so that while they are waiting one of the girls reads from a book to the rest.

THE NEW POWER

One feature which makes an enormous difference is the way in which power is supplied. There are no longer any fires any-where, and therefore no heat, no grime, no smoke, and hardly any dust. The whole world has evolved by this time beyond the use of steam, or any other form of power which needs heat to generate it. There seems to have been an intermediate period when some method was discovered of transferring electrical power without loss for enormous distances, and at that time all the available water-power of the earth was collected and syndicated; falls in Central Africa and in all sorts of out-of-the-way places were made to contribute their share, and all this was gathered together at great central stations and internationally distributed. Tremendous as was the power available in that way, it has now been altogether transcended, and all that elaborate arrangement has been rendered useless by the discovery of the best method to utilize what the late Mr. Keely called dynaspheric force— the force concealed in every atom of physical matter.

It will be remembered that as long ago as 1907, Sir Oliver Lodge remarked that "the total output of a million-kilowatt station for thirty million years exists permanently and at present inaccessibly in every cubic millimetre of space". (*Philosophical Magazine*, April, 1907, p. 493.) At the period which we are now describing, this power is no longer in-accessible, and consequently unlimited power is supplied free to everyone all over the world. It is on tap, like gas or water, in every house and every factory in this com-munity, as well as everywhere else where it is needed, and it can be utilized for all possible purposes to which power can be turned. Every kind of work all over the world is now done in this way. Heating and lighting are simply manifestations of it. For example, whenever heat is required, no one in any civilized country thinks of going through the clumsy and wasteful process of lighting a fire. He simply turns on the force and, by a tiny little instrument which can be carried in the pocket, converts it into heat at exactly the point required. A temperature of many thousands of degrees can be produced instantly wherever needed, even in an area as small as a pin's head.

By this power all the machines are running in the factory which we inspected, and one result of this is that all the workers emerge at the end of the day without having even soiled their hands. Another consequence is that the factory is no longer the ugly and barren horror to which in earlier ages we were painfully accustomed. It is beautifully decorated—all the pillars are carved and wreathed with intricate ornament, and there are statues standing all about, white and rose and purple—the last being made of porphyry beautifully polished. Like all the rest of the buildings, the factory has no walls, but only pillars. The girls wear flowers in their hair, and indeed flowers plentifully decorate the factory in all directions. It is quite as beautiful architecturally as a private house.

CONDITIONS OF WORK

A visitor who calls to look over the factory obligingly asks some questions from the manageress—a young girl with black hair and a gorgeous garland of scarlet flowers in it. The latter replies:

"We are told how much we are to do. The manager of the community cloth-stores considers that he will want so many cloths by such a time. Sometimes few are wanted, sometimes many, but always some, and we work accordingly. I tell my girls to come to-morrow according to this demand—for one hour, or two, or four according to what there is to do. Usually about three hours is a fair average day's work, but they have worked as long as five hours a day when there was a great festival approaching.

"No, not so much because new clothes were required for the festival, but because the girls themselves wanted to be entirely free from work for a week, in order to attend the festival. You see we always know beforehand how much we are expected to turn out in a given week or month, and we calculate that we can do it by working, say, two and a half hours each day. But if the girls want a week's holiday for a festival, we can compress two weeks' work into one by working five hours a day for that week, and then we can close altogether during the next one, and yet deliver the appointed amount of cloth at the proper time.

"Of course, we rarely work as much as five hours; we should more usually spread the work of the holiday-week over some three previous weeks, so that an hour extra each day would provide all that is needed. An individual girl frequently wants such a holiday, and she can always arrange it by asking someone to come and act as a substitute for her, or the other girls will gladly work a few minutes longer so as to make up for the amount which she would have done. They are all good friends and thoroughly happy. When they take a holiday they generally go in to visit the central library or cathedral, to do which comfortably they need a whole day free."

A visitor from the outside world wonders that anyone should work at all where there is no compulsion, and asks why people do so, but meets with little sympathy or comprehension from the inhabitants :

" What do you mean ? " says one of them, in answer, " we are here to work. If there is work to do, it is done for His sake. If there is no work, it is a calamity that it happens so, but He knows best."

" It is another world ! " exclaims the visitor.

" But what other world is possible ? " asks the bewildered colonist ; " for what does man exist ? "

The visitor gives up the point in despair, and asks :

" But who tells you to work, and when and where ? "

" Every child reaches a certain stage," replies the colonist. " He has been carefully watched by teachers and others, to see in what direction his strength moves most easily. Then he chooses accordingly, perfectly freely, but with the advice of others to help him.

10

You say work must begin at this time or at that time, but that is a matter of agreement between the workers, and of arrangement each day."

There is a certain difficulty in following this conversation, for though the language is the same a good many new words have been introduced, and the grammar has been much modified. There is, for example, a common-gender pronoun, which signifies either ' he ' or ' she '. It is probable that the invention of this has become a necessity because of the fact that people remember and frequently have to speak of incarnations in both sexes.

At all the various kinds of factories visited the methods of work are of much the same kind. In every place the people work by watching machines doing the work, and occasionally touching adjusting buttons or setting the machine going anew. In all, the same short hours of labour are the rule, except that the arrangements at the restaurant gardens are somewhat different. In this case the staff cannot altogether absent itself simultaneously, because food has to be ready at all times, so that there are always some workers

on duty, and no one can go away for a whole
day without previous arrangement.   In all
places where perpetual attendance is necessary, as it is at a restaurant, and at certain
repairing shops, and in some other departments, there is an elaborate scheme of
substitution.   The staff is always greatly in
excess of the requirements, so that only a small
proportion of it is on duty at any one time.
The cooking or arrangement of food, for
example, at each of the restaurants is done by
one man or one woman for each meal—one for
the big meal in the middle of the day, another
for morning breakfast, another for tea, each
being on duty something like three hours.

Cooking has been revolutionized.   The lady
who does this work sits at a kind of office-
table with a regular forest of knobs within her
reach.   Messages reach her by telephone as
to the things that are required; she presses
certain knobs which squirt the required
flavour into the blanc-mange, for example,
and then it is shot down a kind of tube and is
delivered to the attendant waiting in the
garden below.   In some cases the application
of heat is required, but that also she does

without moving from her seat, by another arrangement of knobs.

A number of little girls hover about her and wait upon her—little girls from eight to fourteen years old. They are evidently apprentices, learning the business; they are seen to pour things out of little bottles, and also to mix other foods in little bowls. But even among these little girls, if one wants a day or a week off, she asks another little girl to take her place, and the request is always granted; and though of course the substitute is likely to be unskilled, yet the companions are always so eager to help her that no difficulty ever arises. There is always a large amount of interplay and exchange in all these matters; but perhaps the most striking thing is the eager universal good-will which is displayed—everybody anxious to help everybody else, and no one ever thinking that he is being unfairly treated or " put upon ".

It is also pleasant to see, as has been already mentioned, that no class of work is considered as inferior to any other class. But indeed there is no longer any mean or dirty labour left. Mining is no longer undertaken, because all that is needed can be as a rule alchemically produced with much less trouble. The knowledge of the inner side of chemistry is such that almost anything can be made in this way, but some things are difficult and therefore impracticable for ordinary use. There are many alloys which were not known to the older world.

All agricultural work is now done by machinery, and no person any longer needs to dig or to plough by hand. A man does not even dig his own private garden, but uses instead a curious little machine which looks something like a barrel on legs, which digs holes to any required depth, and at any required distance apart, according to the way in which it is set, and shifts itself along a row automatically, needing only to be watched and turned back at the end of the row. There is no manual labour in the old sense of the world, for even the machinery itself is now made by other machinery; and though machinery still needs oiling, even that appears to be done in a clean manner. There is really no low or dirty labour required. There are not even drains, for everything is chemically converted and eventually emerges as an odourless grey powder, something like ashes, which is used as a manure for the garden. Each house has its own converter.

There are no servants in this scheme of life, because there is practically nothing for them to do; but there are always plenty of people ready to come and help if necessary. There are times in the life of every lady when she is temporarily incapacitated from managing her household affairs; but in such a case some one always comes in to help—sometimes a friendly neighbour, and at other times a kind of ladies' help, who comes because she is glad to help, but not for a wage. When any such assistance is required, the person who needs it simply applies through the recognized means of communication, and some one at once volunteers.

PRIVATE PROPERTY

There is but little idea of private property in anything. The whole colony, for example, belongs to the community. A man lives in a certain house, and the gardens are his so that he can alter or arrange them in any way that he chooses, but he does not keep people out of them in any way, nor does he encroach upon his neighbours. The principle in the community is not to own things, but to enjoy them. When a man dies, since he usually does so voluntarily, he takes care to arrange all his business. If he has a wife living, she holds his house until her death or her remarriage. Since all, except in the rarest cases, live to old age, it is scarcely possible that any children can be left unprotected, but if such a thing does happen there are always many volunteers anxious to adopt them. At the death of both parents, if the children are all married, the house lapses to the community, and is handed over to the next young couple in the neighbourhood who happen to marry. It is usual on marriage for the young couple to take a new house, but there are cases in which one of the sons or daughters is asked by the parents to remain with them and take charge of the house for them. In one case an extension is built on to a house for a grandchild who marries, in order that she may still remain in close touch with the old people; but this is exceptional.

There is no restriction to prevent people from gathering portable property, and handing it over before death to the parents selected for the next life. This is always done with the talisman, as has already been said, and not infrequently a few books accompany it, and sometimes perhaps a favourite picture or object of art. A man, as we have mentioned, can earn money if he wishes, and can buy things in the ordinary way, but it is not necessary for him to do so, since food, clothing and lodging are provided free, and there is no particular advantage in the private ownership of other objects.

A PARK-LIKE CITY

Although in this community so large a number of people are gathered together into one central city and other subordinate centres, there is no effect of crowding. Nothing now exists in the least like what used to be meant by the central part of a city in earlier centuries. The heart of the great central city is the cathedral, with its attendant block of museum, university and library buildings.

This has perhaps a certain resemblance to the buildings of the Capitol and Congressional Library at Washington, though on a still larger scale. Just as in that case, a great park surrounds it. The whole city and even the whole community exists in a park—a park abundantly interspersed with fountains, statues and flowers.

The remarkable abundance of water everywhere is one of the striking features. In every direction one finds splendid fountains, shooting up like those at the Crystal Palace of old. In many cases one recognizes with pleasure exact copies of old and familiar beauties; for example, one fountain is exactly imitated from the Fontana di Trevi in Rome. The roads are not at all streets in the old sense of the word, but more like drives through the park, the houses always standing well back from them. It is not permitted to erect them at less than a certain minimum distance one from another.

There is practically no dust, and there are no street sweepers. The road is all in one piece, not made of blocks, for there are no horses now to slip. The surface is a beautiful polished stone with a face like marble and yet an appearance of grain somewhat like granite. The roads are broad, and they have at their sides slight kerb-stones ; or rather it would be clearer to say that the road is sunk slightly below the level of the grass at each side, and that the kerb-stones rise to the level of the grass. The whole is thus a kind of shallow channel of polished marble, which is flooded with water every morning, so that the roads are thus kept clean and spotless without the necessity of the ordinary army of cleaners. The stone is of various colours. Most of the great streets are a lovely pale rose-colour, but some are laid in pale green.

Thus there is really nothing but grass and highly polished stone for the people to walk upon, which explains the fact that they are always able to go bare-footed, not only without inconvenience but with the maximum of comfort. Even after a long walk the feet are scarcely soiled, but notwithstanding, at the door of every house or factory, there is a depression in the stone—a sort of shallow trough, through which there is a constant rush of fresh water. The people, before entering the house, step into this and their feet are instantly cooled and cleansed. All the Temples are surrounded by a ring of shallow flowing water, so that each person before entering must step into this. It is as though one of the steps leading up to the Temple were a kind of shallow trough, so that no one carries into the Temple even a speck of dust.

LOCOMOTION

All this park-like arrangement and the space between the houses make the capital of our community emphatically a ' city of magnificent distances '. This however does not cause the slightest practical inconvenience, since every house possesses several light running cars of graceful appearance. They are not in the least like any variety of motor-car—they rather resemble bath-chairs made of light metal filigree work, probably aluminium, with tyres of some exceedingly elastic substance, though apparently not pneumatic. They run with perfect smoothness and can attain a high speed, but are so light that the largest size can be readily pushed with one finger. They are driven by the universal power; a person wishing to start on a journey charges from the power-tap a sort of flat shallow box which fits under the seat. This gives him sufficient to carry him clear across the community without recharging, and if he wishes for more than that, he simply calls at the nearest house, and asks to be allowed to attach his accumulator to its tap for a few moments.

These little cars are perpetually used; they are in fact the ordinary means of locomotion, and the beautiful hollow polished roads are almost entirely for them, as pedestrians mostly walk along the little paths among the grass. There is little heavy transport—no huge and clumsy vehicles. Any large amount of goods or material is carried in a number of small vehicles, and even large beams and girders are supported on a number of small trolleys which distribute the weight. Flying machines are observed to be commonly in use in the outer world, but are not fashionable in the community, as the members feel that they ought to be able to move about freely in their astral bodies, and therefore rather despise other means of aerial locomotion. They are taught at school to use astral consciousness, and they have a regular course of lessons in the projection of the astral body.

SANITATION AND IRRIGATION

There is no trouble with regard to sanitation. The method of chemical conversion, mentioned some time ago, includes deodorization, and the gases thrown off from it are not in any way injurious. They seem to be principally carbon and nitrogen, with some chlorine, but no carbon dioxide. The gases are passed through water, which contains some solution, as it has a sharp acid feeling. All the gases are perfectly harmless, and so is the grey powder, of which only a little is present. All bad smells of every kind are against the law now, even in the outer world. There is not what we should call a special business-quarter in the town, though certain factories are built comparatively near one another, for convenience in interchanging various products. There is, however, so little difference between a factory and a private house that it is difficult to know them apart, and as the factory makes no noise or smell it is not in any way an objectionable neighbour.

One great advantage which these people have is their climate. There is no real winter, and in the season corresponding to it the whole land is still covered with flowers just as at other times. They irrigate even where they do not cultivate; the system has been extended in a number of cases into fields and woods and the country in general, even where there is no direct cultivation. They have specialized the eschscholtzia, which was so common in California even centuries ago, and have developed many varieties of it, scarlet as well as brilliant orange, and they have sown them all about and allowed them to run wild.

They have evidently in the beginning imported seeds of all sorts extensively from all parts of the world. People sometimes grow in their gardens plants which require additional heat in winter, but this is not obtained by putting them in a green-house, but by surrounding them with little jets of the power in its heat form. They have not yet needed to build anywhere near the boundary line of the community, nor are there any towns or villages for some distance on the other side of that boundary. The whole estate was a kind of huge farm before they bought it, and it is surrounded principally by smaller farms. The laws of the outside world do not trouble or affect the community, and the Government of the continent does not in any way interfere with it, as it receives a nominal yearly tribute from it. The people of the community are well-informed as regards the outside world; even school-children know the names and location of all the principal towns in the world.

CHAPTER VI

CONCLUSION

The Federation of Nations

THE whole object of this investigation was to obtain such information as was possible about the beginnings of the Sixth Root-Race and the community founded by the Manu and the High-Priest for that purpose. Naturally therefore no special attention was directed to any other part of the world than this. Notwithstanding, certain glimpses of other parts were obtained incidentally, and it will perhaps be interesting to note these; but they are put down without attempt at order or completeness, just as they were observed.

Practically the whole world has federated itself politically. Europe seems to be a Confederation with a kind of Reichstag, to which all countries send representatives. This

central body adjusts matters, and the Kings
or Presidents of the various countries are
Presidents of the Confederation in rotation.
The rearrangement of political machinery by
which this wonderful change has been brought
about is the work of Julius Cæsar, who re-
incarnated some time in the twentieth century
in connection with the coming of the World-
Teacher to reproclaim the WISDOM. Enormous improvements have been made in all
directions, and one cannot but be struck with
the extraordinary abundance of wealth that
must have been lavished upon these. Cæsar,
when he succeeds in forming the Federation
and persuades all the countries to give up
war, arranges that each of them shall set
aside for a certain number of years half or a
third of the money that it has been accustomed to spend upon armaments, and devote it to
certain social improvements which he specifies.

According to his scheme the taxation of
the entire world is gradually reduced, but
notwithstanding, sufficient money is reserved
to feed all the poor, to destroy all the slums,
and to introduce wonderful improvements
into all the cities. He arranges that those

11

countries in which compulsory military service has been the rule shall for a time still preserve the habit, but shall make their conscripts work for the State in the making of parks and roads and the pulling down of slums and the opening up of communications everywhere. He arranges that the old burdens shall be gradually eased off, but yet contrives with what is left of them to regenerate the world. He is indeed a great man ; a most marvellous genius.

There seems to have been some trouble at first and some preliminary quarrelling, but he brings together an exceedingly capable band of people—a kind of cabinet of all the best organizers whom the world has produced —reincarnations of Napoleon, Scipio Africanus, Akbar and others—one of the finest bodies of men for practical work that has ever been seen. The thing is done on a gorgeous scale. When all the Kings and prime ministers are gathered together to decide upon the basis for the Confederation, Cæsar builds for the occasion a circular hall with a great number of doors so that all may enter at once, and no one Potentate take precedence of another.

The Religion of the World-Teacher

Cæsar arranges all the machinery of this wonderful revolution, but his work is largely made possible by the manifestation and preaching of the World-Teacher, so we have here a new era in all senses, not merely in outward arrangement, but in inner feeling as well. All this is long ago from the point of view of the time at which we are looking, and the manifestation of the World-Teacher is now becoming somewhat mythical to the people, much as His Palestinian manifestation was to many people at the beginning of the twentieth century.

The religion of the world now is largely that which He founded, though naturally it has been greatly modified as the centuries have rolled by ; that is *the* Religion, and there is no other of any real importance, though there are still some survivals, of which the world at large is somewhat contemptuously tolerant, regarding them as fancy religions or curious superstitions. Everything has been very greatly liberalized, and no one now troubles himself about the religious opinions of his fellows. They are regarded as exclusively his own affair. The universal acceptance of all the great truths which Theosophy taught centuries ago has naturally made for perfect liberty and tolerance ; so fanaticism or interference with the opinions of another would be considered extremely ill-bred.

There are a few people who represent the older form of Christianity—who in the name of the Christ of Palestine refused to receive Him when He came in a new form. The majority regard these people as hopelessly out-of-date. On the whole the state of affairs all the world over is obviously much more satisfactory than in the earlier civilizations. Armies and navies have disappeared, or are only represented by a kind of small force used for police purposes. Poverty also has practically disappeared from civilized lands ; all slums in the great cities have been pulled down, and their places taken, not by other buildings, but by parks and gardens.

THE NEW LANGUAGE

This curious altered form of English, written in a kind of short-hand with many grammalogues, has been adopted as a universal commercial and literary language. Ordinarily educated people in every country know it in addition to their own, and indeed it is obvious that among the upper and commercial classes it is rapidly superseding the tongues of the different countries. Naturally the common people in every country still speak their old tongue, but even they recognize that the first step towards progress in the world is to learn the universal language. The great majority of books, for example, are printed only in that, unless they are intended especially to appeal to the uneducated. In this way it is now possible for a book to have a much wider circulation than it could ever have had before. There are still university professors and learned men who know all the old languages, but they are a small minority, and all the specially good books of all languages have long ago been translated into this universal tongue.

In every country there is a large body of middle and upper class people who know no other language, or know only the few words of the language of the country which are necessary in order to communicate with servants and labourers. One thing which has greatly contributed to this change is this new and improved method of writing and printing, which was first introduced in connection with the English language and is therefore more adapted to it than to others. In our community all books are printed on pale sea-green paper in dark blue ink, the theory being apparently that this is less trying to the eyes than the old scheme of black on white. The same plan is being widely adopted in the rest of the world. Civilized rule or colonization has spread over many parts of the world which formerly were savage and chaotic; indeed almost no real savages are now to be seen.

THE OLD NATIONS

People have by no means yet transcended national feelings. The countries no longer fight with one another, but each nation still thinks of itself with pride. The greatest advantage is that they are not now afraid of one another, and that there is no suspicion, and therefore far greater fraternity. But on the whole, people have not changed much; it is only that now the better side of them has more opportunity to display itself. There has not as yet been much mingling of the nations; the bulk of the people still marry in their own neighbourhood, for those who till the soil almost always tend to stay in the same place. Crime appears occasionally, but there is much less of it than of old, because the people on the whole know more than they did, and chiefly because they are much more content.

The new religion has spread widely and its influence is undoubtedly strong. It has become an entirely scientific religion, so that though religion and science are still separate institutions, they are no longer in opposition as they used to be. As I have said, the fundamental teachings of Theosophy are now universally accepted as the orthodox science of the day, and therefore many of the superstitions which still remained in the twentieth century (such as the doctrines of hell, of the wrath of God and of vicarious atonement) are discredited, and all religions have to modify their tenets to include these scientifically-demonstrated truths. Naturally people are still arguing, though the subjects are not those which we know so well. For example, they discuss the different kinds of spirit-communion, and quarrel as to whether it is safe to listen to any spooks except those who have been authorized and guaranteed by the orthodox authorities of the time.

Schools exist everywhere, but are no longer under the control of the Church, which educates no one except those who are to be its own preachers. Ordinary philanthropy is not needed, since there is practically no poverty. There are still hospitals, and they are all Government institutions. All necessaries of life are controlled, so that there can be no serious fluctuations in their price. All sorts of luxuries and unnecessary things are still left in the hands of private trade—objects of art, and things of that kind. But even with this, there is not so much competition as division of business; if a certain man opens a shop for the sale of ornaments and such things, another one is not likely to start in business close by, simply because there would not be enough trade for the two; but there is no curtailing of liberty with regard to that.

Land and Mines

The conditions as to the ownership of private land and of mines and factories are much changed. In England a large amount at least of the land is held nominally from the King, on some sort of lease by which it reverts to him unconditionally at the end of a thousand years, but he has the right to resume it at any intervening period if he chooses, with certain compensations. In the meantime it may descend from father to son, or be sold or divided, but never without the consent of the authorities. There are also considerable restrictions as to many of these estates, referring to what kind of buildings may be erected on them. All factories for necessaries are State property, but still there is no restriction which prevents anyone from starting a similar factory if he likes.

There is still some mining, but much less than of old. The cavities and galleries of many of the old mines in the northern parts of Europe are now used as sanatoria for the rare cases of consumption or bronchial or other affections, because of their equal temperature in summer and winter. There are also arrangements for raising metal from great depths, which cannot exactly be called mines, for they are much more like wells. This may be considered a modern and improved type of mine. Little of the work is done down below by human beings ; rather machines excavate, cut out huge slices and lift them. All these are State property in the ultimate, but in many cases private owners rent them from the State. Iron is burnt out of various earths in some way, and the material is obtained with less trouble than of old.

THE GOVERNMENT OF BRITAIN

The Government of England has been considerably changed. All real power is in the hands of the King, though there are ministers in charge of separate departments. There is no parliament, but there is a scheme the working of which is not easy fully to comprehend in the rapid glimpse which is all that we had. It is something more or less of the nature of the referendum. Everybody has a right to make representations, and these pass through the hands of a body of officials whose business it is to receive complaints or petitions.

If these representations show any injustice, it is rapidly set right without reference to the higher authorities. Every such petition receives attention if it can be shown to be reasonable, but it does not usually penetrate to the King himself, unless there are many requests for the same thing. The Monarchy is still hereditary, still ruling by the claim of descent from Cerdic. The British Empire appears to be much as in the twentieth century, but it was an earlier federation than the greater one, and it naturally acknowledges permanently one King, while the World-Federation is constantly changing its President. Some of what used to be Colonial Governors now hold their offices by heredity, and are like tributary Monarchs.

LONDON

London still exists, and is larger than ever, but much changed, for now all over the world there are no fires, and consequently no smoke. Some of the old streets and squares are still recognizable in general outline, but there has been a vast amount of pulling-down, and improvements upon a large scale. St. Paul's Cathedral is still there, preserved with great care as an ancient monument. The Tower has been partly reconstructed. The introduction of one unlimited power has produced great effects here also, and most things that are wanted seem to be supplied on the principle of turning on a tap. Here also few people any longer cook in private houses, but they go out for meals much as they do in the community, although things are served here in a different manner.

OTHER PLACES

Taking a passing glance at Paris, it also is seen to be much changed. All the streets are larger and the whole city is, as it were, looser. They have pulled down whole blocks, and thrown them into gardens. Everything is so hopelessly different. Glancing at Holland, we see a country so thickly inhabited that it looks like almost a solid city. Amsterdam is, however, still clearly distinguishable, and

they have elaborated some system by which
they have increased the number of canals and
contrive to change all the water in all of them
every day. There is not any natural flow of
water, but there is some curious scheme of
central suction, a kind of enormous tube
system with a deep central excavation.

The details are not clear; but they somehow
exhaust the area and draw into that all sewage
and such matters, which are carried in a great
channel under the sea to a considerable
distance and are then spouted out with
tremendous vigour. No ships pass anywhere
near that spot, as the force is too great. Here
also, as in the community, they are distilling
sea-water and extracting things from it—
obtaining products from which many things
are made—articles of food among others, and
also dyes. In some of the streets they grow
tropical trees in the open air by keeping round
them a constant flow of the power in its heat
aspect.

Centuries ago they began by roofing in the
streets and keeping them warm, like a green-
house; but when the unlimited power appeared
they decided to dispense with the roofs, about

which there were many inconveniences. In passing glimpses at other parts of the world, hardly anything worth chronicling was seen. China appears to have had some vicissitudes. The race is still there and it does not seem to have diminished. There is a good deal of superficial change in some of the towns, but the vast body of the race is not really altered in its civilization. The great majority of the country people still speak their own tongue, but all the leading people know the universal language. .

India is another country where but little change is observable. The immemorial Indian village is an Indian village still, but there are no famines now. The country groups itself into two or three big kingdoms, but is still part of the one great Empire. There is evidently far more mixture in the higher classes than there used to be, and much more intermarriage with white races: so that it is clear that among a large section of the educated people the caste system must to a great extent have been broken down. Tibet seems to have been a good deal opened up, since easy access is to be had to it

by means of flying machines. Even these,
however, meet with occasional difficulties,
owing to the rarity of the air at a great height.
Central Africa is radically changed, and the
neighbourhood of the Victoria Nyanza has
become a sort of Switzerland full of great
hotels.

ADYAR

Naturally it is interesting to see what has
happened by this time to our Headquarters at
Adyar, and it is delightful to find it still
flourishing, and on a far grander scale than in
older days. There is still a Theosophical
Society; but as its first object has to a large
extent been achieved, it is devoting itself
principally to the second and third. It has
developed into a great central University for
the promotion of studies along both these lines,
with subsidiary centres in various parts of the
world affiliated to it.

The present Headquarters building is re-
placed by a kind of gorgeous palace with an
enormous dome, the central part of which
must be an imitation of the Taj Mahal at

Agra, but on a much larger scale. In this great building they mark as memorials certain spots by pillars and inscriptions, such as: " Here was Madame Blavatsky's room "; " Here such and such a book was written "; " Here the original shrine-room "; and so on. They even have statues of some of us, and they have made a copy in marble of the statues of the Founders in the great hall. Even that marble copy is now considered as a relic of remote ages.

The Society owns the Adyar River now, and also the ground on the other side of it, in order that nothing may be built over there that may spoil its prospect, and it has lined the river-bed with stone of some sort to keep it clean. They have covered the estate with buildings, and have acquired perhaps an additional square mile along the sea-shore. Away beyond Olcott Gardens they have a department for occult chemistry, and there they have all the original plates reproduced on a larger scale and also exceedingly beautiful models of all the different kinds of chemical atoms. They have a magnificent museum and library, and a few of the things which were here at the beginning of the twentieth century are still to be seen. One fine old enamelled manuscript still exists, but it is doubtful whether there are any books going back as far as the twentieth century. They have copies of *The Secret Doctrine*, but they are all transcribed into the universal language.

THE THEOSOPHICAL SOCIETY

The Society has taken a great place in the world. It is a distinct department in the world's science, and has a long line of specialities which no one else seems to teach. It is turning out a vast amount of literature, possibly what we should call texts, and is keeping alive an interest in the old religions and in forgotten things. It is issuing a great series somewhat resembling the old 'Sacred Books of the East,' but on a more magnificent scale. The volume just issued is number 2,159. There are many pandits who are authorities on the past. Each man appears to specialize on a book. He knows it by heart and knows all about it, and has read thoroughly all the commentaries upon it.

12

The literary department is enormous, and is the centre of a world-wide organization. Though they still use English, they speak it differently, but they keep the archaic motto of the Society written in its original form. The Society's dependencies in other parts of the world are practically autonomous—big establishments and universities in all the principal countries; but they all look up to Adyar as the centre and origin of the movement and make it a place of pilgrimage. Colonel Olcott, though working in the community in California as a lieutenant of the Manu, is the nominal President of the Society, and visits its Headquarters at least once in every two years. He comes and leads the salutations before the statues of the Founders.

Three Methods of Reincarnation

As in the examination of the Californian community a great many people were seen who were clearly recognizable as friends of the twentieth century, it seems desirable to enquire how they manage to be there—

whether they have been taking a number of rapid incarnations, or have calculated their stay in the heaven-world so as to arrive at the right moment.

The enquiry leads in unexpected directions and gives more trouble than had been anticipated, but at least three methods of occupying the intermediate time have been discovered. First, some of the workers do take the heaven-life, but greatly shorten and intensify it. This process of shortening but intensifying produces considerable and fundamental differences in the causal body; its effects cannot in any way be described as better or worse, but they are quite certainly different. It is a type which is much more amenable to the influence of the Devas than the other, and this is one of the ways in which modifications have been introduced. That shorter heaven-life is not confined in a little world of its own, but is to a great extent open to this Deva influence.

The brains of the people who come along that line are different, because they have preserved lines of receptivity which in other cases have been atrophied. They can be more easily influenced for good by invisible beings, but there is a corresponding liability to less desirable influences. The personality is less awake, but the man inside is more awake in proportion. Those who take the longer heaven-life focus practically all their consciousness in one plane at once, but people of this other type do not. Their consciousness is more equally distributed on the different levels, and consequently they are usually less concentrated upon the physical plane and less able to achieve in connection with it.

There are others to whom a different opportunity has been offered, for they were asked whether they felt themselves able to endure a series of rapid incarnations of hard work devoted to the building of the Theosophical Society. Naturally, such an offer is made only to those who bring themselves definitely to a point where they are useful—those who work hard enough to give satisfactory promise for the future. To them is offered this opportunity of continuing their work, of taking incarnation after incarnation without interval, in different parts of the world, to carry the

Theosophical Movement up to the point where it can provide this large contingent for the community.

The community at the time when it is observed is much larger than the Theosophical Society of the twentieth century; but that Society has increased by geometrical progression during the intervening centuries —so much so that although practically all the hundred thousand members of the community have passed through its ranks (most of them many times), there is still a huge Society left to carry on the activities at Adyar and the other great centres all over the world.

We have seen already two methods by which persons who are in the Society in the twentieth century may form part of the community of the twenty-eighth century—by the intensification of the heaven-life, and by the taking of special and repeated incarnations. Another method is far more remarkable than either of these—one which is probably applied in only a limited number of instances. The case which drew attention to this was that of a man who had pledged himself to the Master for this work towards the conclusion of his twentieth century incarnation, and unreservedly devoted himself to preparation for it.

The preparation assigned was indeed most unusual, for he needed development of a certain kind in order to round off his character and make him really useful—development which could only be obtained under the conditions existing in another planet of the chain. Therefore he was transferred for some lives to that planet and then brought back again here—a special experiment made by permission of the Maha-Chohan Himself. The same permission was in some cases obtained by other Masters for Their pupils, though such an extreme measure is rarely necessary.

Most of the members of the community have been taking a certain number of special incarnations, and therefore have preserved through all those lives the same astral and mental bodies. Consequently they have retained the same memory, and that means that they have known all about the community for several lives, and had the idea of it before them. Normally such a series of special and rapid incarnations is arranged only for those who have already taken the first of the great Initiations.

For them it is understood that an average of seven such lives should bring them to the Arhat Initiation, and that after that is attained seven more should suffice to cast off the remaining five fetters and attain the perfect liberation of the Asekha level. This number, fourteen incarnations, is given merely as an average, and it is possible greatly to shorten the time by especially earnest and devoted work, or, on the other hand, to lengthen it by any lukewarmness or carelessness. The preparation for the work of the community is an exception to ordinary rules, and although all its members are definitely aiming at the Path, we must not suppose that all of them have attained as yet to the greater heights.

A certain small number of persons from the outside world, who are already imbued with the ideals of the community, sometimes come and desire to join it, and some at least of these are accepted. They are not allowed to intermarry with the community, because of the especial purity of race which is exacted, but they are allowed to come and live among the rest, and are treated exactly like all the others. When such members die they rein-carnate in bodies belonging to the families of the community.

The Manu has advanced ideas as to the amount of progress which He expects the community as a whole to make in a given time. In the principal Temple He keeps a kind of record of this, somewhat resembling a weather-chart, showing by lines what He has expected and how much more or less has been achieved. The whole plan of the community was arranged by our two Masters, and the light of Their watchful care is always hovering over it. All that has been written gives only a little gleam of that light—a partial fore-shadowing of that which They are about to do.

HOW TO PREPARE OURSELVES

It is certainly not without express design that just at this time in the history of our Society permission has been given thus to publish this, the first definite and detailed forecast of the great work that has to be done. There can be little ·doubt that at least one of the objects of the Great Ones in allowing this is not only to encourage and stimulate our faithful members, but to show them along what lines they must specially develop themselves, if they desire the inestimable privilege of being permitted to share in this glorious future, and also what (if anything) they can do to pave the way for the changes that are to come. One thing that can be done here and now to prepare for this glorious development is the earnest promotion of our first object, of a better understanding between the different nations and castes and creeds.

In that everyone of us can help, limited though our powers may be, for every one of us can try to understand and appreciate the qualities of nations other than our own; every one of us, when he hears some foolish or prejudiced remark made against men of another nation, can take the opportunity of putting forward the other side of the question —of recommending to notice their good qualities rather than their failings. Every one of us can take the opportunity of acting in an especially kindly manner toward any foreigner with whom we happen to come into contact, and feeling the great truth that when a stranger visits our country all of us stand temporarily to him in the position of hosts.

If it comes in our way to go abroad—and none to whom such an opportunity is possible should neglect it—we must remember that we are for the moment representatives of our country to those whom we happen to meet, and that we owe it to that country to endeavour to give the best possible impression of kindliness and readiness to appreciate all the manifold beauties that will open before us, while at the same time we pass over or make the best of any points which strike us as deficiencies.

Another way in which we can help to prepare is by the endeavour to promote beauty in all its aspects, even in the commonest things around us. One of the most prominent characteristics of the community of the future is its intense devotion to beauty, so that even the commonest utensil is in its simple way an object of art. We should see to it that, at least within the sphere of our influence, all this is so with us at the present day; and this does not mean that we should surround ourselves with costly treasures, but rather that, in the selection of the simple necessaries of every-day life, we should consider always the question of harmony, suitability and grace. In that sense and to that extent we must all strive to become artistic; we must develop within ourselves that power of appreciation and comprehension which is the grandest feature of the artist's character.

We should be especially on our guard against the insidious and most meretricious cult of deliberate ugliness which the Lords of the Dark Face are at the present time plotting with great skill and subtlety to impose upon our world under the guise of novelty and quasi-progress. Wisdom, Strength and Beauty are essential attributes of the Godhead,— qualities which it is our duty to set before ourselves as an ·example, to endeavour to develop within ourselves so far as may be, and to impress in every possible way upon our surroundings. There is abroad in the world just now a spirit of unrest, of perverseness, of impatience with all that is old, however beautiful it may be, a mad desire for change at any cost, even though it be obviously for the worse.

No sensible man will deny that there is much of wickedness in the world, and that in many respects change is sorely needed ; but discrimination is needed as well. The Powers of Evil are ever eagerly watching for opportunities to do harm, to check our advancement, and so they take advantage of every impulse that can be twisted into a malign direction. We may see their treacherous influence not only in art, whether it be painting or sculpture, but in so-called music, in dancing, in the immoral cult of the macabre and the intentionally crude and hideous. In all these ways and in many more, those who know can see the indications of a vast and carefully-organized conspiracy, all the more dangerous because it so cleverly cloaks its depravity under the disguise of fashion, of novelty, of modernity. Let us at least follow the sound advice of St. Paul : " Whatsoever things are true . . . whatsoever things are pure, whatsoever things are lovely . . . think on these things." (Phil. iv, 8.)

While thus making an effort to evolve the good side of the artistic character, we must carefully avoid the less desirable qualities which it sometimes brings with it. The artistic man may be elevated clear out of his ordinary every-day self by his devotion to his art. By the very intensity of that, he has not only marvellously uplifted himself, but he also uplifts such others as are capable of responding to such a stimulus. But unless he is an abnormally well-balanced man, this wonderful exaltation is almost invariably followed by its reaction, a correspondingly great depression. Not only does this stage usually last far longer than the first, but the waves of thought and feeling which it pours forth affect nearly everybody within a considerable area, while only a few (in all probability) have been able to respond to the elevating influence of the art. It is indeed a question whether many men of artistic temperament are not, on the whole, thus doing far more harm than good ; but the artist of the future will learn the necessity and the value of perfect equipoise, and so will produce the good without the harm ; and it is at this that we must aim.

It is obvious that helpers are needed for the work of the Manu and the Chief Priest, and that in such work there is room for all conceivable diversities of talent and of disposition. None need despair of being useful because he thinks himself lacking in intellect or ecstatic emotion; there is room for all, and qualities which are wanting now may be speedily developed under the special conditions which the community will provide. Good-will and docility are needed, and perfect confidence in the wisdom and capability of the Manu; and above all the resolve to forget self utterly and to live only for the work that has to be done in the interests of humanity. Without this last, all other qualifications " water but the desert ".

Those who offer themselves to help must have in some sort the spirit of an army—a spirit of perfect self-sacrifice, of devotion to the Leader and of confidence in Him. They must above all things be loyal, obedient, painstaking, unselfish. They may have many other great qualities as well, and the more they have the better; but these at least they must have. There will be scope for the keenest intelligence, the greatest ingenuity and ability in every direction; but all these will be useless without the capacity of instant obedience and utter trust in the Masters. Self-conceit is an absolute barrier to usefulness. The man who can never obey an order because he always thinks that he knows better than the authorities, the man who cannot sink his personality entirely in the work which is given to him to do, and co-operate harmoniously with his fellow-workers—such a man has no place in the army of the Manu, however transcendent his other qualifications may be. All this lies before us to be done, and it will be done, whether we take our share in it or not; but since the opportunity is offered to us surely we shall be criminally foolish if we neglect it. Even already the preparatory work is beginning; the harvest truly is plenteous, but as yet the labourers are all too few. The Lord of the Harvest calls for willing helpers; who is there among us who is ready to respond?

C. W. L.

EPILOGUE

IT is obvious that the outline of the Californian community and of the world of the twenty-eighth century is but an infinitesimal fragment of the 'Whither' of the road along which humanity will travel. It is an inch or two of the indefinite number of miles which stretch between us and the goal of our Chain, and even then a longer 'Whither' stretches beyond. It tells of the first small beginnings of the sixth Root Race, beginnings which bear much the same proportion to the life of that Race, as the gathering of the few thousands on the shore of the sea that washed the south-eastern part of Ruta bore to the great fifth Root Race that is now leading the world.

We do not know how long a time is to elapse from those peaceful days to the years during which America will be rent into pieces by earthquakes and volcanic outbursts, and a new continent will be thrown up in the Pacific, to be the home of the sixth Root Race. We see that later the strip in the far west of Mexico, on which the community exists, will become a strip on the far east of the new continent, while Mexico and the United States will be whelmed in ruin. Gradually will that new continent be upheaved, with many a wild outburst of volcanic energy, and the land that was once Lemuria will arise from its age-long sleep, and lie again beneath the sun-rays of our earthly day.

It may be supposed that a very long period will be occupied by these great seismic changes, ere the new land will be ready for the new Race, and its Manu and its Bodhisattva will lead it thither.

Then will come the ages during which its seven sub-races will rise, and reign, and decay; and from the seventh the choosing of the germs of the seventh Root Race by its future Manu, and the long labours of that new Manu and of His Brother the new Bodhisattva, until it shall, in turn, grow into a definite new Race and inherit the earth. It also will have its seven sub-races, to rise, and reign, and vanish—vanishing as the earth itself falls asleep, and passes into its fourth obscuration.

13

The Sun of Life will rise on a new earth, the planet Mercury, and that fair orb will pass through its day of ages, and again that Sun will set and the night will fall. A new rising, a new setting, on the globes F and G of our Round, and the ending of the Round, and the gathering of its fruits into the bosom of its Seed Manu.

Then, after long repose, the fifth, sixth and seventh Rounds, ere our terrene Chain shall vanish into the past. Then, onwards yet, after an Inter-Chain Nirvana, and still there are fifth and sixth and seventh Chains yet to come and to pass away, ere the Day of the High Gods shall decline to its setting, and the soft still Night shall brood over a resting system, and the great Preserver shall repose on the many-headed serpent of Time.

But even then the 'Whither' stretches onward into the endless ages of Immortal Life. The dazzled eyes close; the numbed brain is still. But above, below, on every side, stretches the illimitable Life who is GOD, and in Him will ever live and move and exist the children of men.

PEACE TO ALL BEINGS

A. B.

INDEX

Printed by A. K. Sitarama Shastri, at the Vasanta Press. Adyar, Madras.

LaVergne, TN USA
16 September 2009
158039LV00002B/25/A